RUNNING AGAINST THE WIND

By Arthur R. Bracke
for
Robert J. Bracke

Cover Art By Norel M. Lemaire

Note for Librarians: A cataloguing record for this book is available from Library and Archives Canada at www.collectionscanada.ca/amicus/index-e.html

ISBN 1-4120-8209-9

Printed on paper with minimum 30% recycled fibre.
Trafford's print shop runs on "green energy" from solar, wind and other environmentally-friendly power sources.

Offices in Canada, USA, Ireland and UK

Book sales for North America and international:
Trafford Publishing, 6E–2333 Government St.,
Victoria, BC V8T 4P4 CANADA
phone 250 383 6864 (toll-free 1 888 232 4444)
fax 250 383 6804; email to orders@trafford.com

Book sales in Europe:
Trafford Publishing (UK) Limited, 9 Park End Street, 2nd Floor
Oxford, UK OX1 1HH UNITED KINGDOM
phone 44 (0)1865 722 113 (local rate 0845 230 9601)
facsimile 44 (0)1865 722 868; info.uk@trafford.com

Order online at:
trafford.com/05-3175

10 9 8 7 6 5 4 3 2 1

Running Against The Wind
An Early Biography of R. Bracke

TABLE OF CONTENTS

Chapter One

Busted

My workday was nearing its end. My thoughts were now of Annette and the long drive home. Even though we had only been seeing each other for a short while, I was already beginning to have a genuine need to have her there beside me. What made this girl so different from all the rest was that I felt absolutely safe and comfortable telling her all of my innermost secrets. I was finally able to talk to someone about all of the horrors that I experienced as a young child in foster care and I could even share the truth about what I am doing now. No, I'm not talking about my apprenticeship at a world-class restaurant in Williamsburg, VA, I'm talking about my *other* life, the life of a drug dealer, and the *real* reasons behind that.

I had just left the restaurant for home when Annette called me on the car phone. She told me about a great party that would be happening later and I told her that I would be by to pick her up after I showered and changed.

It's not like Annette is the only girl I've ever been crazy about. Actually there've been quite a few. I especially remember one who I met back in Middle School, right after I came to live in Virginia where I was about to be adopted. There was this girl named Mary something who transferred to my school near the end of the seventh grade. Since I had already tried to hook up with most of the other girls at school but just not having found the right one, I thought that I would try to get to know her and see what she's all about. We were able to hit it off right away. She had been through some of the same things that had tormented me also, like coming from a broken home and having to move to a strange area not knowing anyone there and having to start all over again. We really didn't get into that much because I never really saw her outside of school. And then came the long summer when I didn't see her at all. When school began again in the fall, it wasn't long before she had to move away.

Annette and I got to the party around nine that night and were practically inseparable the entire time. What a party! Drugs were plentiful and alcohol flowed freely and we had our share of both. All of my friends were there and all of us were expecting to party through the night, until morning.

Suddenly the man of the house appeared and we all had to leave without having a chance to sleep it off.

We had just left the party with a couple of Annette's girlfriends tagging along. After dropping her and them off, I was heading home feeling pretty wasted but good at the same time. After all, in my "circle of friends", I was Paco, "Big Dog" – wheeling and dealing drugs, you name it, I could get it.

So here I was driving home at 11:00 PM, cruising down Route 33, intoxicated and reeking of alcohol, with thoughts of Annette and her girlfriends running through my spaced-out mind. It was December 28, 1997. I had just turned twenty years old a month earlier. I was floating on a cloud, thinking how lucky I was to have Annette, my customized 300-ZX, and on top of it, pockets full of cash.

All of a sudden, I heard a siren. Looking into the rear view mirror, I saw flashing blue lights coming up behind me fast. As instinct kicked in, I automatically put the pedal to the metal and the car shot forward and hit ninety before I knew it. Adrenaline started rushing through my body, adding to my confusion. I was trying to hang on to the steering wheel at the same time I was rolling the windows down and frantically searching for the drugs I'd stashed in the car earlier that evening, then throwing the little baggies out the window. Oh, did I need to get rid of *them*!

This wasn't cool at all. After all, I knew that I couldn't keep it up forever, but why did it have to happen right now? Just when my life seemed so complete with Annette and all of my so-called friends and "cool acquaintances". Here I was weaving all over the road trying to get rid of contraband before the officer could catch me. In the confusion, I was almost killing myself at the same time I was dumping the drugs and trying to outrun the flashing blue lights that seemed as though they were inside my car and my doped-up brain. I had to get away. And there were still more drugs hidden somewhere in the car.

Something kept reaching out for me from both sides of the road, whipping at my car, scaring the hell out of me. It took a while until I realized it was the long branches of old willow trees lining the roads that seemed to be waving and beckoning me to stop be fore I killed myself or someone else. I was running out of gas anyway, so I pulled over to the side of the road and came to a screeching halt. The deputy sheriff's car came careening in right behind me and almost rear ended me. I was busted!

The deputy blinded me with his flashlight so that I could barely see the tip of his gun. "Out of the car, hands on your head!" A demanding voice ordered me to face my car. I had barely stepped out of the vehicle before I was slammed up against it, spread-eagled, patted down and handcuffed. In a gruff voice, the deputy announced, "I clocked you at speeds up to 92 miles an hour . . . and I saw you throwing those baggies out the window!"

The deputy had his hands all over me, down both sides of my body, my chest, my crotch, my inner thighs, all the way down to my ankles, my back and my butt, searching for any kind of weapon. He came up empty handed, but his "back-up", who had just arrived, acted like he'd just found Fort Knox.

"Let's take him down to the office," the other deputy hollered out.

All I could think of was Annette. Why didn't I listen to her earlier? All this because of a stupid hat I'd left at the party. If I hadn't decided to turn around to go back to get it, I'd have been home by now. Okay, it wasn't just the hat - it was the drugs, too. I thought I was so cool. I was oblivious to the harm I was causing to families, especially to young people. Even though I was cooking at a four-star restaurant, I wanted more money! Selling drugs became my way of making it, and competition was never a problem. I was damn good at what I did. Now this – all because of my stupidity, here I was being shocked back to reality by a deputy sheriff of Middlesex County, Virginia.

The deputy ushered me into the back seat of his patrol car while the other one picked up as many of my discarded baggies as he could find. I felt like this was going to be the end of the world as I knew it. My body became weak and I thought I was going to pass out. Less than an hour later, the humiliation continued when they placed me in a holding cell at the jail. I waited for my turn to let the jail officer strip search me, as they do all felony suspects. Next came the fingerprinting, and after that, the officer came back to the holding cell, took my clothes, and issued me one sorry looking, ill fitting, ugly orange jumpsuit. With it, I received a piece of paper listing all the charges against me, including D.U.I., reckless driving and possession of marijuana with intent to distribute.

Annette and I had been smoking rock cocaine for the better part of the evening. We were both dizzy and numbed by the drugs we'd shared, which, of course, impaired our judgement. I soon realized that this whole affair was like a nightmare I couldn't wake up from, when one of the guards walked up to the front of the holding cell, looked through the bars at me, and asked if I wanted to make a phone call. I could make a call to arrange for a bail bondsman, he said; it was the law – each and every inmate was allowed to call family or a bail bondsman to secure bail.

Next, I was placed in the Pink Room. This was a holding cell that was painted pink in order to calm inmates, so that we wouldn't get depressed about being in jail and try to commit suicide or harm other inmates. It seemed as though, while sitting in the Pink Room in my ugly orange jumpsuit waiting for orientation, my whole life started going through my mind in sequence, as though I were reliving all the events that had occurred to me as far back as I could remember.

When my mother couldn't afford to keep me and placed me in foster care in Florida, that's when all the bad stuff started happening in my life. I was just an innocent little kid, like all children when they're that young. These bad memories were engraved in my mind; there was no escaping my terrible past, no matter how desperately I tried to overcome the nightmare that had taken hold of me at such an early age.

All of a sudden, one of the not-so-nice guards shook me, wanting to know if I'd had any luck in securing bail. That thought was wishful thinking because, in reality, I was alone, all alone. The only person on this earth who would feel any sympathy towards me now was Annette, because she's the only one who *really* knows what I'm all

5

about. She knows about the drugs and how I'd worked so hard to keep that part of my life from my dad.

Nevertheless, I decided to face the music and try my dad – well, actually my adopted father, the man who'd legally adopted me and brought me to Virginia when I was twelve. By then, I had already been bounced in and out of several foster homes, some good, some not so good; the abuse had started for me at a very early age, at the hands of a couple of really mean foster parents.

As I dialed my dad's number, ready to explain I was in jail, I started getting this real empty feeling in the pit of my stomach. I remembered his stern admonition: "I will not bail you out of jail if you're ever locked up for alcohol or drug related offenses - you know better." As these words played over in my mind, it was all so déjà vu. This time, the phone rang for what seemed an eternity, until finally my dad picked it up. I realized then that "No" meant "No". I slid the receiver back on the hook with the question of my freedom along with it. He really did mean no!

My dad, who works for the county Department of Social Services as a social worker and a child abuse investigator, was very familiar with these types of situations that helped to ruin the lives of young adults who tried their hand at making a fast buck. I understood the tough love he was now giving me. But, to me, the timing was all off; tough love wasn't what I needed right now. While pondering my resources, I thought of Annette again and decided to give her a call to see if she could help me. I wanted out of jail!

I thought back to the day Annette and I first met. I was checking my pager when a phone number appeared with 911 attached to it. As a rule, I normally ignored such calls, but this one I saved to phone back the next day. One of the sweetest voices I'd ever heard answered – it was as if I was talking to an angel. Annette introduced herself, then went on to explain that the previous day's call came because one of her friends had been trying to buy drugs from me. I knew then that I had to meet this girl. I arranged a date with her and the rest is history.

Waiting for Annette now to pick up the phone seemed like an eternity after the first couple of rings. She finally answered in her sweet angel voice, as if she were sleeping, with a slight rasp to the "Yes", that she greeted me with.

I tried to stay calm as I briefed her I was in jail for a D.U.I. and possession of a controlled substance with intent to sell, but I was getting excited. And she could tell. She told me not to worry. Her voice sounded so responsible and confident as she assured me that, of course, she's do everything possible to get me out on bail, that I should just sit tight and not worry. We even started to find some humor in the situation, and laughed about a few things before we said, "Bye."

Still, I felt like a hopeless convict, utterly helpless, waiting minute by minute for a guard to call out my name and tell me to roll it up. Annette was my only true friend and I had no choice but to count on her, to place all my trust in her. But at the same time, my gut feelings made me nervous when I thought about her age. Annette was only fifteen, even though, at times, I credited her with the maturity of someone much older. Unsettled, I lay back on my small, confining jail-house mattress, waiting for my bail to be posted, as I drifted into a disturbed sleep, with the noise of gates slamming shut as the officers booked new inmates into the jail.

Morning came only too soon, and with it the realization that I was still behind bars. I also had one of the worst hangovers going on and I felt like shit! It was a wonder I was still alive after all the reckless driving and the police chase the night before, not to mention the drugs I had done at the party. I even snorted some heroin. Boy, was I glad I didn't have any of that on me when I finally pulled over and surrendered. The sheriff's deputies had already spooked me for a drug dealer. As I lay on my mattress thinking just a bit clearer about my situation, a guard pushed a metal tray under my cell door. Breakfast – a couple of dry pieces of toast and some pasty, thick oats that I had a hard time swallowing.

I had just finished eating the slop when another officer came to interview me. After all questions were duly asked and answered, I was shuffled off to a "dormitory". When the officer assigned me my bunk, I took a look around to check out the facilities. I felt like I was back in school with a bunch of my old classmates. There were quite a few familiar faces here, just like old home week! What a noisy place and, needless to say, no privacy whatsoever.

I settled down on my bunk as a group of my "boyz" ambled over and started with the bullshit. Among them was one of my real tight buddies, Reggie. "Man, how come they got you down?" Reggie wanted to know, and "Are you gonna get out?" The dude was downright elated that I had now joined him in the ranks as a fellow convict. I looked at Reggie in a way to just let him know I was tired of all the shit, and returned with a "I hope the hell I do."

The rest of the boyz wanted in on the happenings, wanted to know how and why I'd been busted. I began with the party and all the fine babes who were there. The police chase was next and, as I continued, I noticed the adrenaline rush become contagious among the younger inmates listening, while a few of the old timers responded with a "I've heard that one before", as though they'd already been through the same thing by now in their lives of crime. Reggie wanted to know what the babes were wearing, how much they were wearing and who was showing the most skin.

The crowd had started to thin out by the time the conversation got around to my bail and who was posting it. I told Reggie I'd already called Annette, my lady, and was now just waiting for one of the officers to tell me to roll it up, because Annette had told me not to worry about a thing, to leave everything in her hands and I'll be out real soon.

Reggie chuckled, then intimated, "Man, that slut ain't gonna bust a grape."

A few of the boyz overheard our conversation and also took it upon themselves to start calling Annette everything but a child of God. I came to her defense, telling these assholes to chill and get off my lady's case.

The loudspeaker came on while we were shooting the shit. One mean-sounding officer was instructing everybody to stand in front of their bunks for evening count before the lights went out. The block came to order in what seemed like a nanosecond as everybody scurried to their respective bunks. A peaceful quiet came over the place; loud voices lowered to a hush, while two big buffed guards strolled past, counting inmates to make sure no one had escaped, telling each of us, one by one, to grab a bunk, lights out.

I tried for a long time to fall asleep in this cage full of other people who had committed an array of different crimes, but this joint just lacked privacy, which took some getting used to. Annette was back in my dreams when I finally succumbed to sleep. I was getting out; Annette was waiting by the release area ready to take me home. But

9

then I also dreamed about what a messed up childhood I had had before we met. It wasn't easy to let go of the past, to just forget all about the bad stuff that had happened with our parents. I kept having nightmares about my birth mother, how hard it seemed for her to try to love me, to even touch me.

I couldn't manage to wake up the next morning until I was rudely shaken by Reggie, telling me to rise and shine for morning count. What, another count? I couldn't believe it. We hadn't even had breakfast, and the guards were already checking to see if some inmate had been lucky enough to escape in the middle of the night.

The food on that second day left a lot to be desired; it was equally as bad as the first day's crap when that officer had slid the tray under my cell door. Small comfort that, this time, at least we were let out to go to the chow hall, which gave me a chance to see who else was locked down with me. I could hardly believe my eyes. It seemed as though half of my high school crowd was in jail with me for drugs or robbery. The guards made sure to rush us in to eat the slop they served, so that nobody would have time to complain, which would have been a waste of time, anyway. So we were in and out in a matter of fifteen minutes.

The moment I settled in, back in the block, I got in line for the phone and waited my turn to call Annette and see what was taking her so long to post my bail. I needed to know if she was going to get me out, or would I have to sit and wait until my trial came up, which was still over a month away. The bigger the inmate, the longer they stayed on the phone, pushing smaller, less fortunate inmates to the back of the line to wait till last for their turn.

Finally, I dialed Annette's number and anxiously waited for her to answer. Her sweet voice came over the line. Boy, was I glad to hear that! But as soon as she started speaking, I could tell she'd been drinking, and drinking quite a bit. Her speech was slurred as she told me she was having a hard time trying to get a bail bondsman to listen to her as an adult. Everyone she called would end up hanging up on her because they thought that she was just playing games on the phone. I begged her to please keep trying, and for God's sake to sober up before she tried calling anyone else.

When I returned to my bunk, Reggie came running over with some baby powder and asked if I wanted to smoke. I looked at him in a real crazy way, and waited to find out just what we were going to smoke. I had smoking pot on my mind. What a great escape that would have been.

Reggie unscrewed the top of the baby powder can and pulled out some contraband cigarettes. A couple of our buddies went to the shower area and started steaming up the place so that the guards who passed by in the hallway couldn't tell the smoke from the steam. While we were indulging ourselves, another inmate wandered over to our group and asked if anyone wanted to buy a piece of a twenty-dollar rock.

This fool had cut off a piece from a bar of soap and was now jokingly trying to pass it off as rock cocaine. We all started laughing at the soap. The nurse passed medications out three times a day to a few of the inmates in my block, which would provide another opportunity to get some type of high. This medication consisted of Motrin and cold medicine and, if enough were ingested at one time, they could produce a high or slightly altered state.

The excitement ended; no one was caught smoking cigarettes, which was pure luck because they were illegal to have in jail, and if you were caught with them it would mean another charge. Such charges were occasionally filed against those unlucky ones who got busted smoking, only because the smell of the baby powder wasn't strong enough to kill the smell of the cigarette smoke.

I lay back on my bunk day dreaming about Annette and my bail and with thoughts of freedom ever on my mind. I wanted out of this jail, and by the end of my second day, I was really starting to get scared. I couldn't even use the toilet in privacy, what with over twenty others looking me in the face. Annette told me she needed an adult to guarantee the remainder of the bail, and I knew my dad still wouldn't have anything to do with it, so asking him again was out of the question.

I started thinking about Sam, a man I'd met one night while I was hanging out with some of my buddies. Sam was cool, and a good deal older than my underage buddies and me. Sam would buy us alcohol and smoke crack with us. One thing led to another, and Sam became Annette's mom's new boyfriend. As an ex-con, Sam just might be sympathetic to my having to spend New Year's Eve in jail.

I dozed off right after count was finished and the guards left the area. I dreamed of Annette and Sam coming to my rescue, bailing me out of this hellhole. The sooner the better. I had a much better chance of fighting these charges from the street.

Chapter Two

Rude Awakenings

My second night in jail, with nothing but spare time on my hands, all I did was daydream and escape into my thoughts. At least twenty or more other bodies were in the block with me and the place smelled like a locker room after a football game. The noises of gates slamming shut and the chatter of the others throughout the night kept disturbing me, interrupting my sleep and the dreams I kept going back to as I'd fall asleep again. It seemed like the more I was disturbed, the deeper my dreaming became. In my dreams I had gone all the way through my life as a young adult and back to the time when horrible things were happening to me as a very young child.

I finally had the chance to have a normal loving father when the man who really adopted me eight years earlier made everything legal and final, and now I had to go screw it up playing with drugs. My dad had taught me better, a lot better than this. My dad was the only person on earth who really cared about my welfare and my future. Everyone else somehow had bailed out on me, and by now I'd lost complete track of my biological family.

The cards that life had dealt to me sucked. I had come from a broken home at a very early age. It all began when my biological dad started having an affair and decided to stop helping my mother pay the bills and support two little boys. I was told that my mother didn't like touching me much and that she was kind of afraid of me. When I was

13

born, three years after my older brother, Raymond, I was blamed for coming along and ruining everything for my folks. Of course in reality, that wasn't the case.

My mother couldn't handle the responsibility of caring for two small children by herself while doing drugs. My folks were married in January 1973, and had my brother, Raymond, two years later, on January 29, 1975. I was born nearly three years later, on November 16, 1977. Then, when I was only two or three months old, our trailer was destroyed by fire. After that, it took my folks a couple of years to get back on their feet again. Later on, my dad used to tell me how Raymond had rescued me from the burning trailer, but in actuality, I learned that dad had started the fire himself in order to get the insurance money. It was only about a month later when my dad decided to start playing around on my mom with a younger woman. Three months went by before my folks split up as a result of my dad's wandering. My mom gave Raymond to her parents to keep and two months later, when I was only eight months old, she placed me in foster care with the state, which placed me with the Cinelli family, where I stayed for the next ten months.

By the time I got to the Cinellis' home, I was underweight and malnourished. My mother had just stopped paying attention to me, leaving me at the nursery for days at a time while she was busy doing drugs. I ended up staying in foster care until I was eighteen months old and then my dad went to court and won custody back. He was also able to get my older brother back and, a few months later, he married the young girl he had been cheating on my mom with, before they separated and our family fell to pieces. It was June 1979, when we all got back together, except my mom. She was replaced by a woman named Janet. Janet was good to my brother and me over the next three years. It was like she was always there for us while my dad was away. During these times my dad was busy getting a criminal record and we didn't matter much to him. Now my life has become just like the old saying, like father, like son.

I was talking in my sleep when I felt Reggie shaking me awake, telling me it was morning, chow time. "Wake up so they can get the morning count over with", Reggie was saying, "so then we can go eat."

I couldn't wait to tell Reggie everything I'd just tripped about. It seemed so real, just like it was happening to me all over again. "Reggie, man you'll never believe all the crap I just went through", I said. This fool wanted to know if she was any good. Reggie wasn't a very serious person and I would have probably just wasted my time telling him anything.

On my third day in jail I let one of the "brothers" locked down with me talk me into dreadlocks. So now I had blond dreads, which made me feel more like I was one of the cons. I also made an ankle bracelet out of wool threads, which I unraveled from a coarse blanket, so I was sportin' a piece of jailhouse jewelry along with the dreads. I was starting to fit in with the jail house scene and the rest of the guests; I'd stopped worrying so much. Nevertheless, I still anticipated my bail being posted.

The third day in jail really seemed to drag on. That's when I decided to give my dad one more call. I knew deep down inside that he'd probably say no again, but what the hell, I had nothing to lose, and by some wild stretch of the imagination, he might just do it.

I dialed the number with cautious optimism. My hopes, of course, were shattered as soon as my dad answered and told me no. He went on to remind me about the talks we'd had in the past about drugs, how destructive they were and how I should stay away from them. And then the final blow: "When this is over, if you ever decide to play around, drinking and driving or messing with drugs again, don't even bother to call me." He said good bye and hung up the phone.

That was that. What a way to spend New Year's Eve. I went back to my bunk kicking myself in the ass, thinking about the mess I'd gotten myself into. I had nothing but time on my hands as I waited and started to trip on life and my lady, Annette. I thought about all the money I'd spent on her and how I would buy her whatever she wanted. Some nights I'd spend at least three to four hundred dollars on her, easily. I was counting on her heavily, to raise the bail.

Later that evening, we were in the chow hall having dinner, when a bad fight broke out between two of the inmates. One of them pulled a makeshift knife on the other dude and was trying to stab him just as the guards ran in and broke it up. An authoritative voice came over the loudspeaker, telling us to put our hands over our heads where they could be seen, then to file slowly out into the hallway one by one in single file, and go straight back to our block for a count.

On our way back, the guards hurried by us in the hall, dragging the dude who had the knife down the hall in handcuffs on his way to a solitary cell ("the hole"), while he cussed them under his breath. Meanwhile, the other dude was busy trying to talk *his* way out of the hole. He had the attention of one of the senior officers, who was listening to his side of the story.

The minute we got back to our block, the officers started walking through for what I thought was just another count. Reggie whispered over to me to watch out, that this was no regular count, that these officers were considered the goon squad and that they would probably shake us down and search for contraband. They left the block as quickly as they came, without incident and, before we knew it, it was count time again.

That third night in jail, I had plenty of time to do some soul searching and to daydream about the past. I went back to the time when I was a young kid. I was back in Florida, waiting for the rest of my family to wake up. Oh, I was so excited. My dad was very generous, and always made sure we kids had a nice Christmas. In my dreams everything seemed so real, as I waited for everybody to get up so we could open the presents. But when the family finally got up and we opened the presents, the boxes were empty. These dreams seemed so real, and they would just go on and on all night long. But my dreams had turned into nightmares. In one of them I was waiting, pacing back and forth outside a jailhouse, looking for my dad, whose police record kept increasing with each passing year of my life. It started with D.U.I.'s, breaking and entering, burglary, contributing to the delinquency of a minor, hit and run, obstruction of justice and possession and sale of rock cocaine.

I would wait around for my dad's release so that we could go to his produce stand to sell to people who were buying more rock cocaine from him than produce. I'd see my dad standing behind the counter, an evil smile on his face, telling his customers to come back, that next time it would be better. Then the police would show up and take all of his money and haul him back to jail. My dreams were so bad that sometimes I couldn't wake up from them, and there was no stopping them. When this happened, the dreams of my abuse memories prevailed, ad infinitum.

My step-mom's boyfriend also beat up on me after my dad decided to leave again. Janet's boyfriend would beat the living hell out of my big brother and me every chance he got. My dad got wind of what was happening while he was away playing house and decided to take my brother and me back. This gave us a chance to move again and was exciting for us. By now we'd lived in every flea-ridden hotel in South Florida amongst the lowlifes and derelicts from every walk of life you could imagine.

The memories of my grandmother's house were always sad ones. The sounds of toilets flushing in the background from inmates relieving themselves in the middle of the night made my nightmares all the more real, as I ran into the bathroom in my grandmother's house to hide from my uncle. I loved my dad's younger brother, and so did all the neighborhood girls. I looked up to him because of this, and wanted to be just like him when I reached sixteen. But he had a mean side to him as well, and sometimes he wasn't very nice when he played with my brother and me. The toilet flushing on my head while my uncle held it down in the bowl scared the hell out of me. I woke up to realize that the sound of the toilet flushing was a normal part of life in the block. As I lay back wiping sweat off my brow, thinking about the weird dream I was having from the stress off being in jail, the dreams started again, and I drifted into a restless sleep with my uncle stuffing me into the trash can.

When my dad was in jail, the rest of the family abused us, including my step-grandfather, who once got in on the action by throwing me around the bedroom like a maniac, just because his birds got out of the cage and flew around the house. There was a swimming pool in my grandmother's back yard, which soothed a lot of the abuse and made living with my family there a lot nicer.

It was shortly after my uncle put my head in the toilet that I was hospitalized for a viral infection, and ended up staying in a room by myself for a few days while they injected me with medicine. This hospital was one of the nicest places I can remember staying as a kid.

It wasn't long before my dad was released from jail again, to move my brother and me around one more time to live with his girlfriend, Jan, who was still just a kid herself. We lived with Jan and my dad for a couple of years before that, too, fell apart. Jan ended up being pretty nice while it lasted, and life was back to normal until my eighth birthday rolled around, when my dad made me drink a bottle of Jack Daniels whiskey to celebrate. Talk about sick – it's a wonder I didn't end up with alcohol poisoning! My dad's excuse for doing something this stupid to me was that he was trying to teach me a lesson so that I wouldn't drink any more. From that day on it was real easy to drink liquor without getting sick. My brother and I would sneak my dad's beer into the garage and have our way with it. We always got away with it because the adults were too busy to pay attention to what we were doing.

The nightmares of my past abuse were still going when Reggie shook me awake for morning count and chow. I didn't share my thoughts with him because he was too busy telling me about all the babes he'd just dreamed about. Meanwhile, I kept thinking about how screwed up my life had become over the last forty-eight hours. Jail seemed to be the story of my life for now; that was all I could think about as I chowed down more jail house slop.

Christmas had just come and gone, leaving me tripping about the time shortly after the stay at Jan's house when we ended up in another flea-ridden motel with my dad.

It was just Raymond, my dad and me, and one day my dad didn't show up at our room for dinner. There was a knock at the door. One of the ladies who sometimes fed us was there to see if my brother and I had had anything to eat. This neighbor ended up helping us out while my dad stayed in jail, this time for attempted robbery. My dad and one of his friends had held up a gas station in the area and were busted in the act.

I thought about how Raymond and I went to school and took care of ourselves for a few months before the authorities found out we were alone. Around Christmas time my brother and I went out and stole a tree to put up so that we could celebrate Christmas. The neighbor lady helped us, and also kept our secret. As I thought about my dad and his career as a criminal, the old adage "like father, like son" again preyed upon my mind. I thought about all the time my dad had spent behind bars. My dad was also a police informant who had worked undercover for a drug task force. Hell, it was the only way he could save his ass, especially after having been arrested four times for possession of cocaine with intent to sell. It's a wonder he *ever* had a chance to see us kids. After a few months, my dad was released, but not in time to save us once again from the state and the foster care system. There had been reports of two abandoned boys living in a motel room by themselves.

This time our foster care experience would give us a rude awakening. It didn't take long before we were placed, together again, in the home of an African-American family named Smith, smack in the middle of the projects. Ours were the only white faces around for miles, and we would have to run like hell when we got out of school, or all of the other kids in the neighborhood would beat us up for being white. My family life with the Smiths left a lot to be desired, especially at dinnertime. All I ever remember eating there was black-eyed peas and rice in a back room, while the Smiths' ate real food in front in the dining room. They also had an older son who sold crack cocaine while his dad sold Poli-Pops to the neighborhood kids for a small profit. I hated life at the Smiths' and couldn't wait to be put into another home. As I thought about all of these horrible times, I really tripped. When my dad got out of jail he showed up for crack cocaine at the Hunters', buying it from their son, and leaving my brother and me behind after his purchase.

Reggie was asking if I was okay. I was daydreaming on my way back to the block. It was obvious things were starting to bother me, as I headed back to my bunk, thinking about Annette and getting out of jail. Less than a minute passed after I sat down on my bunk, when an officer showed up at the front of the block and called my name out: "Bracke (pronounced "brock"), Robert Bracke, roll it up. Your bail has been posted!"

Chapter Three

The Homecoming

Happy New Year! Could this really be true? Bailed out at last! I followed the officer to the processing area where I received my clothes. I couldn't wait to find out who had posted my bond. Did my dad have a change of heart? Did Annette finally con somebody into thinking that she was of age?

When I finally got to the lobby, no one was there. Could it all be a big mistake? No, this couldn't be happening! Maybe I could call somebody to find out. Maybe one of my buddies on the outside knew what was up. I asked permission to use the phone but was denied. They ushered me out of the door into the "sally port" and the steel door slammed shut behind me. Then the huge chain-link gate rolled open and I stood there, free at last!

It was New Year's day, I had just been bailed out of jail and nobody was there to meet me. I was wearing shorts and a tee shirt in the forty-degree morning, wondering what to do next. I walked to the gas station in Saluda and begged the attendant to use the phone. At first, she said no, pointing to the pay phone just outside. I explained to her, that I had just gotten out of jail and didn't have any money or anywhere to go. This must have touched a nerve and she handed me the phone but warned me that it was for local calls only. I called this dude, Mac who formerly occupied my position in the dealer hierarchy in my community. Even though there was this smattering of "bad blood" between us, I decided to give him a try.

Mac was surprised to hear from me but was quite sympathetic as he, too, had experienced the indignity of incarceration previously. He would be right there to pick me up. As I waited there for Mac to pick me up, I saw his mother drive by. I wondered what was up because I knew that they only had that one car between them. Could it be that he still held a grudge against me? I waited for about an hour and nobody came. Then the sister of one of my boyz drove up and I asked her if she could hook me up with a ride home.

First she took me to her house where I talked with her brother, Chris. He told me about, how in the past couple of days Annette was taking my situation very hard. He said that she had tried to take her mom's Jeep someplace and drove it into the side of her house. Apparently she had called some of my boyz to help her get it unstuck and they all told him how she'd been pretty well tore down (impaired). Then his sister announced that she was ready to take me home and we left.

As we arrived in our driveway, I was unsure about the greeting I would get. I was afraid that my dad would tell me to get the hell out because, I'm sure, he must have been very disappointed in me. After all, it was barely a month since he had found a quarter pound of marijuana on me and I had promised him, then, that I would never use or deal the stuff again. But he didn't understand how hard it would have been for me to stop, considering that I had four grand in my back pocket and I felt like "everyone" was depending on me. But, boy was I wrong!

As I approached the front door, I saw my dad standing there. I couldn't believe it when he opened the door and said: "Welcome home." He wondered when and how I'd gotten out of jail and how I'd gotten home. I told him and he asked me why I hadn't called him. After, all, it was just the bail he wasn't willing to do, not the ride home.

I couldn't wait to talk to Annette, but no one was home. Anyway, I was home at last. Home, where you get to eat real food; home, where you can shower any time you want to; home, where you can take a shit without an audience! I popped a beer and drank it in the shower. What a way to celebrate the New Year!

At last, my angel answered her phone. We couldn't wait to get face to face. I told her that my car was still at the impound lot. No problem, she would send her mother's boyfriend, Sam, to pick me up.

After a while, Annette's mom's Wagoneer, with her mom, Sam, a girlfriend of her's and that girl's boyfriend appeared in our yard. As I jumped into the Jeep, she whispered in my ear, not to mention where my car was, in front of her mom. Her mom was really impressed with my new hairdo, the dreadlocks!

Back at Annette's house, we went straight to her room and watched videos. We were on the couch. Finally, I had a chance to hold my baby in my arms. The other couple, Ginny and Marty, were on the floor. Marty wanted to know all about how it was in jail. I told him that it was basically like summer camp but without the arts and crafts, and there wasn't a pool. But I had one big question on my mind, who got up my bail? Could it have been Jimmie, who still owed me for two ounces that I fronted him on the night I was arrested? She said, no, no, because every single time that she called him he would avoid the subject. Then she told me that, in desperation, she had called Clarence, "a wanna-be-playa", and promised him that I'd hook him up with a quarter pound of marijuana for the three hundred dollars, which I needed for bail, if he'd front the money.

Sam was the one who delivered the money to the magistrate and he signed the security note for the bondsman. In return, Sam would get eighty dollars worth of "rock" cocaine from me. What a plan! She really used her head on that one! Suddenly, Sam stormed in and told us that we had to leave. He wasn't actually mad, he was just "cracked" up. This really sucked! After all of the time that I've spent missing the hell out of Annette, now it had to come to an abrupt end. Then he took Ginny, Marty and me home.

My first night in my own bed, but I knew that it wouldn't last. I knew that I was probably facing at least a five-year stretch or maybe ten and how unbearable it would be to have to live without Annette for so long. And how would I pay my dad for all of the phone bills and the money he had lent me for cars in the past, and I still had to bail out my car, not to mention Clarence and Sam.

The next day, my dad had to be in court on business. He talked to the prosecutor and explained to him that my car was actually titled jointly to him and me and would he consider releasing it. He agreed to release it but we still had to pay the towing and storage fee of two hundred and twenty dollars. That afternoon we went to retrieve the car and I couldn't believe my eyes. The car was wrapped up like a Christmas present, with "Crime Scene" tape all around it. Everything on the inside, even the moldings, had been removed and searched. The speakers were lying on the seats and there was marijuana all over the seats and the dashboard! When they towed it, they had used the four-way-flashers and did not even bother to turn them off. Now the battery was dead. We had to beg the lot attendant to borrow a battery because jumping it would not do the job to get it started.

As soon as I got the car home, I "decontaminated" the interior and then took off to pick up Annette from one of her girlfriend's homes. She told of a party at a nearby beach so we went there but it was too cold outside. So the party went inside and everyone greeted me with my street name, "Paco", acting like I was still "the man". They all wanted to know when I would be back "in business". At that time, I told them that it would take me a couple of days to renew my connections in Newport News but that I would be ready to hook them up very soon. Annette did not seem to share my enthusiasm, as she gave me a very disapproving look. She seemed to be able to look right into my head. She could tell that the dealing I was doing wasn't just for the money, but that it was as much for the bold and somewhat reckless image that I was portraying for my friends, as anything. All night long I cradled her in my arms and enjoyed her sweet warmth against my body. When Annette's curfew neared, I had to take her home. As we were leaving, everyone told me to come back, because the party would go on until morning.

On the way home, Annette pleaded with me to go home, too, as I was already pretty well ripped. I kissed her good night and went back to the party anyway. I had actually thought twice about it, but in the end I felt that I was just on borrowed time anyway, so what did I have to lose? Around midnight, the lady across the street, who was the same one who hosted the party the night I got busted, came over and invited us to come to *her* house. By now, the group had whittled down to eight, so we accepted her invitation. We took what little beer was left, with us. Suddenly, she appeared with a half gallon of vodka, which she offered to all. Then she told me how bad she felt about my getting arrested after leaving her party last week.

We searched in vain for a shot glass. All we could find was a "Winnie The Pooh" baby glass. So we decided that, up to Winnie's ass was a "shot". I started by taking a shot and issued the challenge for anyone to match me. The only contender was Will, my close friend since the seventh grade. We've really had some crazy times together. Once, on a camping trip with the church youth group, he stole the gum ball machine out of the campground's recreation hall. One night we broke into the local racetrack and ran his GTO around the track at over one hundred and sixty miles an hour, drinking beer and throwing the cans out of the window. Anyway, Will and I were head-to-head for a while but then he finally fell out in a chair in the living room. I decided not to let the rest of the bottle go to waste, so I killed it. Inevitably, what goes in must come out, so I struggled to the bathroom. That's when the room began to spin around and, when I returned to the hallway, I had to steady myself by holding on to the wall. I scanned the living room for a safe place to land and I saw that the couch was unoccupied. That's where I stayed until morning.

When I woke up, the events of the previous night were just a blur. I went to get into my car to go home but it was gone. A couple of guys who had left the party early had taken my keys and moved the car as a joke. Actually, they took the keys because they were afraid I would try to drive the car last night.

Eventually I made it home and took a shower. By now the phone was already ringing from people wanting to know when I could supply their needs. The cops had confiscated my pager as evidence so, shortly after renewing my connection with my source in Newport News, I obtained a new one. After all, I couldn't have my friends calling my house night and day asking me to "hook them up", because that would have really made my dad suspicious. So they would call my pager and I would return their calls on the cell phone in my car. Then I went to Sam's ex-wife's house where I met up with his daughter, Shelly, and Annette. Annette appeared upset. I asked her what was the matter, and she said that she was upset because I was still dealing drugs. I reminded her that she would never have met me in the first place if it hadn't been for her friend's, drug habit and that all she really wanted me for now was the prestige of the money and the status. She said that, at first that had been true, but that, now, her feelings for me had grown into genuine affection. So I promised her that I would try to get out of it as soon as possible, thinking the whole time that it would be impossible, at least for now, since this whole affair had cost me my apprenticeship. She gave me a hug and a kiss good-bye and I went up the road to the home of "D-Man", a guy who had bought "bud" from me in the past. I needed a stake to reestablish my cash flow and I knew that he would front me some money because he has done so in the past. Reluctantly, he fronted me fourteen hundred dollars for a pound of marijuana.

When I got to Newport News, I was able to impress my connection that business was still going strong. But first I had to dispel the rumors they had heard that I'd wrecked my car and they wanted to know what I had been busted for because I had been reluctant to discuss such matters over the phone. I explained to them that I had only been busted with three ounces of bud and that I was charged with D.U.I. So they reassured me that I would come through it okay since it was only my first offense. So we made the deal. I was able to purchase a pound and a quarter with the money.

When I returned to Deltaville, to D-Man's house, I left his pound in his van in his yard because he and his family had gone to bed. Then I went to the home of a girl who I often hung out with and met several people who were waiting to buy from me. I sold the quarter pound at one hundred and twenty five dollars an ounce and ended up making five hundred dollars that night. It was a good night's work but I was really becoming apprehensive because, I knew that sooner or later I was bound to get busted again and then I would surely lose Annette for real.

Chapter Four

The Set-Up

The next morning, Annette told me that Sam had a proposal for me. She said that he had a friend, Jerry, who wanted to buy twenty pounds of marijuana a month for eleven hundred dollars a pound. This deal sounded way too good to be true since I was buying it for eight to nine hundred dollars a pound. I thought that she wanted me to cut back, and now, here she was trying to get me in deeper. Something just didn't add up. At the same time, I knew that Sam was taking her to Newport News to get rock for both of them and that he was stealing from her mother and pawning the items.

Even though we had both promised each other that we would try to get off drugs altogether, it seemed like she was talking out of both sides of her mouth, but now I understand that she was very much under Sam's control. Not only was he addicted to crack, he was also interested in her, sexually. He even tried to pimp her out on one of the crack runs to Newport News. And when this was finally reported to the authorities, he fled the area, but more about that later.

I really had a hard time with this proposal. I waited until the next time I met with my connection in Newport News to discuss it further. I wanted his opinion on this. He thought that it was mighty strange that, after my recent arrest, that somebody out of nowhere expected me to come up with that kind of weight. I went on to tell him that Sam is Annette's mother's boyfriend and that he'd always been cool and, anyway, he's an addict, so he couldn't possibly be a cop. Finally, we agreed that it seemed okay so I went back to Sam and told him that I could hook his friend up.

I was at Annette's house when Sam said that he was going to meet Jerry, a tugboat captain, on his boat to get messed up. I stayed behind with Annette who was home alone while her mother was at work in Richmond. Finally, the long anticipated moment had arrived. We made love for hours and, before I knew it, my pager was going off. It was Sam calling. He wanted me to meet him somewhere on Route 3 in half an hour and he said, sarcastically, "don't be having sex with Lora's daughter." When I hung up, I told Annette that this whole deal just didn't click. When I got up to get dressed, Annette pleaded with me not to go, but I told her that I had promised, and that was that. Anyway, I needed the money because I still didn't have a real job. When I left, she was in tears, which really made me feel guilty and selfish.

When I arrived at the appointed place, Sam was with Jerry in Jerry's SUV. Sam came to my car and told me there was someone whom he wanted me to meet. I walked over to the vehicle with Sam and he introduced us. Jerry showed me twenty–two thousand dollars in one-hundred-dollar bills. Somehow, he already knew that I didn't like large amounts of money in twenty-dollar bills. We agreed to meet that night at "Hooters", a restaurant on Jefferson Avenue in Newport News, to make the deal.

That night, after dinner, I told my dad I was going over to Annette's for a while. I got to Hooters around 8 PM. There I met with Sam and Jerry. There was a waitress at the table when I arrived but they sent her away when I got there. Then Jerry brought up the subject of the deal and showed me the cash again. I explained to him that he needed to give me the money and that I would be back with the bud in less than five minutes. He

31

said that he was not that sure that he could trust me with that kind of money. I tried to explain that I am Annette's boyfriend and that Sam would certainly vouch for my honesty. Then he suggested that Sam should come with me to check out the bud and then we would come back here to get the money and finish making the deal. I said, "Hell no", because there was no way I was going to make it possible for my source to be set up. Then they made me call my connection several times to see if there was any other way he would agree to make the deal. After several hours of haggling, I became very uncomfortable with the whole thing and I backed out.

When I finally got back home, I got a page from Annette. I called her right back and she told me that Sam said that I had screwed up the whole deal because I wouldn't go through with it.

A couple of weeks later, Sam told me that Jerry was ready to deal and, this time, we would do it *my* way, but that he only wanted to buy a pound. By now I'd been to court on the D.U.I. charge and my license had been suspended for six months. Sam eagerly offered to drive me to meet with Jerry.

The next day, several people contacted me wanting to buy. I told them that I just needed a ride to Newport News to pick up the stuff. I called Sam and told him that I had a ride and that I would just meet him at Hooters. There were four of us and all were looking forward to the trip and to the reward at the end. On our way, we stopped at a convenience store and bought four eighteen-packs of beer.

We were on our way. First, we went to Hooters where we met Sam and Jerry in the parking lot. We were all already pretty drunk. Sam jumped into the back seat of our car to ride along. Without any further thought, we took him with us. We went to the apartment complex across the road and I told the driver to park on the other side of the buildings. Everyone gave me their contribution and I took my backpack and I walked the long way around to get to my connection, Clint's, apartment. When I arrived at the apartment I had a beer and handed over the cash. Clint handed me the bud and I put it in the backpack and left. When I got back to the car, I handed everyone their share and I tried to give Sam Jerry's pound but he refused to take it and insisted that I should give it to him because I'm the one who Jerry needs to be dealing with. Then he wanted a "commission" of a hundred dollars, so I threw it to him.

Back at Hooters, Jerry was standing outside at the pay phone and Sam said that we could use his (Sam's) car to finish the deal. As Sam was opening the car door for Jerry, I saw him slide the one-hundred-dollar bill to him. When Jerry and I were in Sam's car together, I pulled the pound of bud out of my backpack and laid it in his lap. As he was looking it over, he remarked that he noticed a lot of stems and seeds and that, he felt, the quality wasn't all that great. At the time, I didn't realize that all of this talk was just his attempt to get me to talk a whole lot about this and to get me to incriminate myself, because, as I found out later, he was wearing a body mike and was recording the whole thing. We made the deal, I got my money and he got his bud. I stepped out of the car and walked over to the car where my buddies were waiting and as I settled in, I cracked open another beer and thought to myself, "I just stepped into a whole lot of shit."

Chapter 5

The Calm Before The Storm

In the days that followed, I tried my best to turn my business over to others who had admired my game for so long. First, there was Bill, who was always eager to go along with whatever was going down at the time. Then there was Mac, the dude whose business I'd taken over when he was concentrating more on his girl and her wishes than on taking care of business. Finally, there was Lana, a girl who seemed to need money desperately. At the same time, I saw more and more of Annette and our relationship became ever more intense.

Because I had lost my license to drive, it was very risky for me to drive to Annette's house, but that never stopped me. Through our devotion for each other, we were able to support one another through the difficult times surrounding the side effects of kicking our respective habits. At the same time, we were in denial about the reality of my situation, the fact that I was facing five to ten years in prison.

Meanwhile, Annette's mom, Lora, came to realize that I was twenty years old and dealing drugs. Her boyfriend, Sam, had moved in with her and had her convinced that he is an undercover cop and that he and his associates were hot on my trail, planning to bust me, big time. Lora, believing this, tolerated me hanging around her daughter because she believed I would soon be back behind bars.

One night, one of Annette's girlfriends decided to throw a party while her parents had gone out. She had made it very clear to me that her mother had told her that I was never to be allowed at her house. Her mom had even called my dad and Lora and told them the same thing. The reason that her mother was so set against me was because, one night a few of us had gotten together at her house while her parents were having a party. We were all upstairs in this girl's room. We wanted some beer so Annette called Sam at the pizza joint where he worked and asked him to bring us some. Sam complied and one of the other guys snuck it upstairs. Eventually, the girl's mom walked in, saw the empty cans and immediately assumed that I had brought the beer. All of us were under age to purchase beer.

So I drove to the party, but only to pick up Annette. When I arrived, everyone was glad to see me except the hostess. I tried to explain to her that I wasn't planning on staying, that I had only come to pick up Annette. That was cool with her, but, she said, if her mom should happen to come home, she'd be dead.

From there, Annette and I went to a secluded beach where we lay in love for a time and mused the possibilities of spending the rest of our lives together, provided, of course, that our feelings would survive my pending incarceration.

The next day, Bill called and wanted to know if I would help him get a quarter pound of marijuana for a friend of his who had given him four hundred dollars. This was the night before my trial for the charge of possession of marijuana with intent to distribute. I figured that this was a really dumb thing for him to be asking me, considering how much trouble I was already in. I decided to talk it over with Annette. She seemed to understand. Besides, we both felt that I deserved a night out with my boyz before getting locked up for five years or more. It made perfect sense at the time.

My dad was starting to notice that I seemed to be making plans to go out and, of course, he didn't think that it was such a good idea, what with court the next day and all, even though he had no idea what I was really up to. Anyway, Bill got a ride to my house so that he could drive my car, since we had to go clear to Newport News and I didn't want to risk getting stopped.

When we got to Clint's house, we were disappointed because he didn't have any bud. This was the first time that I'd ever gone there without telephoning first. Clint tried to reassure me that the next day wouldn't be so bad, that I'd probably get a minimal sentence because, after all, I was just a first offender.

Next, we decided to visit another possible source, a friend of Bill's called "Stick Man". A girl named Renae answered the door and said that Stick had gone out but that he would be back after a while. Bill had a fake ID, so we went to a Food Lion store where he bought a couple of cases of beer. After a while we went back to Stick's place. This time the guy from school, Jimmie, who still owed me two hundred and fifty dollars, was there also.

We took the beer and went inside. Jimmie was complaining about financial problems, like this made any difference to me. I just wanted my money. He didn't stay around long. Stick tried everyone he knew, in order to get us the bud we needed but no luck. Finally, however, he was able to score some cocaine, which he offered to Bill. Uncertain, Bill decided to accept three hundred dollars worth of the white stuff, after all, he said, "This is gonna be your last night out for a while."

Stick was gone about thirty-five minutes. When he returned he had what Bill wanted. Renae supplied a mirror, Bill used his fake ID to cut the lines and I rolled a twenty into a tube and we drank and snorted until around 3:00 AM. We had eight beers left in the fridge, which we took along for the ride home.

On the way home, Bill suddenly realized that he had just spent four hundred dollars that wasn't even his. I had told him about an incident that had supposedly happened to me where I was holding a pound of marijuana for someone when I came up on a police road check with drug-sniffing dogs and how I had thrown the bud out of the window to avoid discovery. I told him that, after I cleared the road check, I hid out until the cops had gone and then I went back to get the pound but it was gone. Bill wanted to know if this was really true, because everyone really had their doubts. Actually, I had had good intentions on that other occasion. I had been given fourteen hundred dollars to buy a pound for D-Man but when I got to Clint's he didn't have any. That time, I really needed the money because I wasn't working anywhere legitimately and I had bills to pay so I made up that story and it stuck. Bill ended up telling his friend the truth and promised to pay him back when he could.

I got home in the wee early hours and quietly slipped into my bed. In what seemed like moments later, my dad was waking me up to get ready for court. I dragged myself out of bed, took a shower, put on my best suit and left with my dad. He dropped me off in front of the courthouse, wanting nothing at all to do with the situation.

This is country court. Middlesex County, VA has six and one-half court days per month. First I had to sit through several hours of traffic court, strung out from the night before. My case was finally called at 11:30 AM.

I rose from my seat in the gallery and approached the judge's bench, my heart racing and my head spinning. Then, to my great amazement, the prosecutor announced that he was requesting that the trial be postponed because the laboratory analysis of the "alleged" marijuana had not yet been received. A new date was set for the following month. I don't even remember how I got home after court, but somehow I did.

All in all, I had really wished that they'd gotten the damn thing over with, because now I had to psyche myself up all over again.

Before court, I had given Annette my pager to keep for me. Now I wanted it back. Apparently, Sam had it and was intercepting the calls, even calling me on the phone on one occasion to tell me that someone had put the message: "911" ("emergency") after their number. I told him that I really didn't care *who* was calling at the time.

A couple of days later I finally made it to Annette's house and it seemed like she didn't want to give the pager back. She seemed afraid that some of the numbers stored in it were people who wanted me to hook them up. I told her to just go ahead and clear the memory because I really had no intention of doing any more dealing.

Things had calmed down considerably and I was actually spending some meaningful time with Annette. Each morning, as soon as I got up, I found some way to get over to her house where I would stay until her mom kicked me out. Frequently I would even cook dinner for them. We spent many hours together, lying in each other's arms, on the couch in her bedroom.

Chapter Six

Enter: "The Governor's Task Force"

Sam continued to persist in trying to get me to get still another pound for Jerry. I was really reluctant to do this since I had stopped dealing drugs altogether. Annette had mentioned that she had found a note of Sam's which listed the names of the others who were along that night when I bought the other pound for Jerry. This just seemed too weird to be innocent. Even Annette thought it was strange.

Against my better judgement, I decided to do it anyway, just this one last time. After all, it was only a couple of days until Valentine's Day and I needed money for some roses for my lady.

We decided when and where we would do the deal. Then, on the night before the deal was to happen, Sam and Annette picked me up and took me to her house. That's when Sam produced a crudely fashioned foil "bowl" (marijuana pipe) and offered us some "hits" (puffs). Annette declined, but I accepted. Somehow, this seemed to be Sam's way of trying to win my trust.

The next morning I was just coming out of the shower when my dad asked me if I knew anyone who owned a blue car. I said: "Maybe. Why?" He said that a blue car had just been in our driveway, sounded it's horn and, after a minute or so, left. Then, he said, he had been monitoring his police scanner and had heard the following conversation:

"The boy ain't home, so I'm going to his girlfriend's house to give him a page." This conversation didn't sound like the usual police business one hears on such a scanner, and my dad was really suspicious.

Almost immediately, my pager lit up, and it was my girl's number! Now, suddenly it all made sense. Sam must be setting me up, big time, trying to get enough on me to have me sent away for life, and Lora must be in on it too. This really scared me, so I called my lawyer. His only advice was that I should not commit any more crimes. At the same time, my pager continued displaying Annette's number, over and over again.

I made up some excuse to take the dog for a romp in the woods behind our house where I had some vodka stashed. The pager was still buzzing! I was worried that, if I don't answer, they might come and raid the house. In my mind, I was rehearing what my dad had told me some time ago: "If the police *ever* find it necessary to search *my* house for something *you* did, you will never be able to live here again!"

After taking several gulps of courage, I came back into the house and called the number. Sam got on the phone and asked me where the hell I'd been. I told him that I had been asleep and then he said that he'd meet me at the end of our lane, because, one time before, my dad had chased him off with a gun. My dad had said that he couldn't understand why a forty-three-year-old man had such an interest in his twenty-year old son.

I told my dad that I really didn't see any other choice and that I was going to meet Sam to see what he would say when I confronted him.

I met Sam as agreed and he wanted to know if I had called Clint yet. I told him no. He didn't want to take a chance on a wasted trip, so he took me to a pay phone to make the call. When we got to the phone, I had trouble remembering the number (I think that the vodka had something to do with it), so Sam dialed the numbers and handed me the phone. Then he got back into his car and pulled away a short distance as if not wanting to be privy to the conversation. Clint answered. I had talked with him on the phone earlier and told him that I thought that something just wasn't right and that the heat could be on him very soon. In other words, "His block was hot." I had suggested that maybe he should go to visit his parents in Richmond for a while. Now I wondered why he hadn't left yet. Concerned that the call was being overheard, I devised a simple code that I knew Clint would understand. I asked him if what we had discussed earlier (his getting out of town) was still cool. Before he could explain, I cut him off and said , "That'll be straight" and hung up the phone. Anyone listening in would have assumed that I was referring to the drug deal not the fact that I had tipped Clint off.

Back in the car, Sam asked me if I smelled oil burning. I said: "No, I smell bacon." (A sarcastic reference to pigs/police officers.) He shrugged that off and we drove toward the far end of a little-used parking lot where Jerry and another man were waiting in Jerry's truck. Sam pulled his car up beside Jerry and they talked. Jerry asked me where I'd been all day and wanted to know if the deal was on. I asked him: "Well, don't *you* know?" He just shrugged. Then, just for the hell of it, I asked him if they were all a bunch of cops. He hesitated for a moment and then he said: "Where we come from, people take offense by such a question." Then he stepped out of his truck and walked around Sam's car, to the side where I was sitting and, as my hands were on the dash, I was telling him that I really didn't want anything to do with this deal. And he said:

"Well, it's there, ain't it?" I said, "Well, I guess", and he threw eleven hundred dollars onto my lap. He got back into his truck and left and Sam and I left for Newport News.

On the way, I kept telling Sam that I needed beer so he stopped a convenience store in Mathews County. In the parking lot, I handed him one of the hundred-dollar bills but he handed it back, saying that *he* would pay for the beer. He returned from the store with a twelve pack and we were back on the road.

On the road, I told Sam that I had the whole thing figured out, that they were obviously all a bunch of cops. So he asked me what that meant. Did it mean that I was cooperating or what? I said: "Yea, I guess." That's when he reached up onto the visor and turned off his pager. That's when he told me how glad he was that I had made this decision because he knew how much I cared for Annette and that he really loved her mother, Lora, and now he and I would be working together, just like one, big, happy family. Then he reached up and, apparently, turned his pager back on.

When we were passing the bowling alley in Gloucester, a green Blazer behind us flashed it's lights and, when we stopped at a light, Sam jumped out of the car and ran back to talk to the driver. When he returned to the car, he didn't mention anything about it and we proceeded on our way to Newport News as I continued to guzzle down the beer.

On Route 17 in Yorktown, Sam pulled into a McDonald's restaurant where he told me to get out of the car and asked me for the money. I wouldn't give it to him and walked into the restaurant with it still in my pocket. I was dumbfounded. What was going to happen next? I left the restaurant by the door on the other side of the building where I noticed two groups of three men each, including Sam, approaching me from opposite directions. Sam said: "I thought you'd probably try to make a run for it." Then they escorted me to the other side of the parking lot where they placed me in the back seat of the Blazer, the one that had flashed its lights at Sam in Gloucester, and proceeded to question me.

They seemed agitated that I knew that they were cops. They wanted to know how I found out. Did Sam tell me? Was there another informant who tipped me off? I explained to them, that I started to figure it out when my dad overheard that conversation on his scanner, and it's been getting more obvious ever since. I had some questions, too. What could happen to me if I chose not to cooperate? What, exactly, was it they wanted me to do? Shouldn't Sam be in trouble for buying me beer?

That's when they advised me of the new charges that were pending against me for possessing and distributing (to an undercover officer) that pound of marijuana at Hooters and for several counts of conspiracy to obtain and distribute a controlled substance. They said, however, if I chose to cooperate, they would see to it that the prosecutor would look more kindly on my situation and would probably "lose" some of the charges. At the time, "cooperation" simply meant that I would not reveal their true identities and the fact that they are all undercover cops. Also, they told me that after it's all over, they would help me relocate and to find new living arrangements, etc.

After *what's* all over? Now it began sounding more like they wanted to "work" me to get to Clint and anyone else in Newport News who was worth getting. They were after the "king pins" but they needed dealers like me to get to guys like Clint and to get to *his* connection, and so on.

This went on for several hours in the McDonald's parking lot. Then one of the officers wanted to know if I thought that Clint would be suspicious if I didn't show. I said that it really wouldn't be cool to ask for a pound and then not get it because that could hurt my reputation with him. So I called him from the pay phone. He said he had just sold the pound to someone else but that he could have more in a couple of hours. I told him OK and hung up but the officers made me call him back and tell him to forget it for now.

On the way home, Sam told me how much he believed I would come to enjoy this. That's when he showed me that his "pager" is not really a pager at all, rather it is a wireless transmitter and that the receiver is located in another vehicle. Now I knew how my dad had accidentally picked up Sam's conversation earlier that day. Sam also seemed really psyched by the fact that he seemed to be above the law.

Chapter Seven

Revelation

Sam took me home. As soon as I walked in, my dad wanted to know how it went. I told him that I got busted, big time, but that I wasn't going to jail just yet. Then I explained to him how the task force wanted to use me to bust Clint by making "controlled buys." This really seemed to trouble my dad as he thought that I could easily end up dead if something went wrong. After all, a narc is held in about as much esteem by this crowd, as cops and child molesters are.

I went into our game room and called Annette. The conversation was real brief. She wanted to know how it went; she wanted details. I told her that I couldn't tell her over the phone and that I really had to talk to her, face to face. I asked her mom's permission if I could come over tonight. Annette hesitated because, she knew, her mother hated my guts. Finally, she asked her anyway and, to our surprise, she said yes! She said that Sam could pick me up in a little while.

Sam was right on time. On the way to Annette's house he wanted to make damn sure that I never told anyone about his involvement with the task force, especially Annette because his daughter, Shelly, was Annette's best friend and, he believed, that if it ever got around to Shelly, that she'd hate him for life. Ironically, I already knew at the time, that he'' been taking the girls to a crack dealer so that he could gain their confidence to

45

get those dealers busted also. He told me that the task force really wasn't interested in me, that what they really wanted was to bust the dealers who were trading crack for sex with under-age girls. They would get them hooked on the stuff and, before they knew it, they owed large amounts and the only way to pay was to get extremely hurt or to give sexual favors.

Back at Annette's, I immediately went with her to her bedroom, upstairs. We settled down on her couch to watch TV. That's when I broke the news to her, about Sam. She was incredulous. I told her the whole story, everything that had gone down that day. She listened in disbelief but never interrupted. Finally, I explained to her, that the only reason I was even considering this was to be with her. Because, the first time I was in jail, it was hell not being able to be with her. So I told her of the "promises" made to me by the task force. It seemed like the only reasonable thing to do at the time. She agreed and we rationalized how this would be the start of our future together.

We held each other for the rest of the night until Lora called up from downstairs, explaining to Annette that Sam was too drunk to take me home so I had two choices, either walk home or stay in the guest bedroom. Of course, Annette wanted me to stay.

When I awoke, Sam was standing beside the bed. He was anxious to know if I had said anything to Annette. He seemed relieved when I told him no. He went on to say what a great lady Lora is and that she could probably help me find a job and get reestablished.

Shortly, Sam and Lora left and went their separate ways, leaving Annette and me behind. When they returned, Sam cooked dinner and insisted that we come down and eat with them. During dinner, it was hard to play along with Sam's bullshit because he was just pretending that everything was normal.

We hadn't been back upstairs long when Sam busted in and gave me an ultimatum. He said that he would either take me home or to a party, which was going on at Lana's house. Annette suggested that I should go ahead on to the party since I hadn't had a good buzz since I found out about the task force.

All of my boyz were at the party, shouting my name: "Paco! Paco! Paco"! They wondered where I had been for the past couple of days. I told them that I'd just been hangin' with Annette. I cracked open a beer and had just sat down when there was a pounding on the door and a loud voice was saying: "Paco, get your ass out here" and "If you don't come out, I'll come in and get you." It was Sam. Everyone was wondering what the hell he wanted. One of my friends went to the door and told him that I'd be out in a minute. I guzzled down my beer and walked to the kitchen and snagged three more. I stuck two into the pockets of my jacket and opened the third. In my mind, I couldn't figure out what the hell he wanted now. When I got to the door, he was half way back to Lora's Jeep. Then I noticed that Lora was there also and Annette. I got into the back seat with Annette and noticed a case of beer on the seat between us. That's when Sam explained that we all needed to sit down and have a talk. Lora agreed.

On the way back to her house, Annette explained that she really didn't want them to come and get me from the party but that she had gone off on her mom, knowing that Sam had been trying to set me up all that time. She said that Sam had actually picked her up and slung her over his shoulder and slammed her into the wagon to come and get me.

We arrived at Annette's house as I was finishing the third beer from the party. I had to carry her into the house because she didn't have her shoes. Once inside, Sam put the case of beer into the fridge and brought out four. We were all in the living room when he began to explain to all what he had told me earlier when he drove me home from being busted. But this time he went further, explaining that he didn't wear a bulletproof vest and that he didn't carry a badge or a gun. He said that this is why he is so very vulnerable and that no one can know what he does, especially his daughter, Shelly. Annette questioned how this could be true, since she had been with him when they were both smoking crack together and there was no way that he could have switched it. But he insisted that, what he was smoking, was only baking soda and that it snaps and pops "just like the real thing" and it even smells like it.

It was clear to me that Sam had been using Annette as a "prop" to gain crack dealers' confidence when he was making controlled buys in Newport News. I asked Lora how she could have ever let Annette be used in that way, especially, considering how Annette had just recently gotten out of a hospital where she was trying to detox from crack. Her reply: "How *else* do you get the dealers?"

Sam interrupted, saying that he didn't believe that I was dyslexic. He handed me a magazine and wanted me to read from it, out loud. I gave it my best shot. It must have been pretty funny. He still didn't believe it but we were all getting pretty tired. Lora had given Annette some kind of pill earlier and she was getting pretty spacey. They debated on where I should sleep and Sam said that, he believed that I would be a "gentleman" if I stayed in Annette's room. Lora had her doubts but she felt that Annette would pass out as soon as her head hit the pillow. All in all, I think that they were both using Annette and me to get what *they* wanted. He wanted to make money and she was desperate for love.

The next morning, Annette's memories of the previous night were vague. She could not remember past the moment that her head had hit the pillow. She asked me if the part about my dyslexia was true. I couldn't lie to her, even though this has been a source of humiliation for me ever since I can remember. So I told her that, yes, it was really true, and she just had to put me to the test. She pointed to a poster on her wall and asked me to read it to her. I recognized the caption and was able to "read" the words almost correctly. That's when she said, "You *can* read" and I said, "Not very well" and she said that she'd like to help me learn to read better. I told her that it was harder for me than she thought. My dad spent a whole summer, between the sixth and seventh grade, trying to teach me, using "Hooked on Phonics", but it didn't help at all.

Out of nowhere, my pager lit up. I called the number and it was "Jerry", one of the task force members. He wanted to know if we could get together for a talk. Feeling that I had no choice, I agreed. He said that he would pick me up shortly.

It wasn't long before the green Blazer with heavily tinted windows appeared in the yard. I got in and we were off to somewhere. There were two agents in the car, but not Jerry. They were talking to Jerry on the radio. We ended up at a volunteer fire department station in Waterview where two other agents joined us. We settled down at a folding table and everyone, but I, had a legal pad.

One of the agents, Barney, had a tape recorder. Jerry told him not to use it because, then, he would have to transcribe the conversation, word for word. They proceeded to ask me all about my dealing history and wanted to know just how long I had known Clint. I told them that I had known him less than a year, not as long as they had thought. Then they wanted to know how I had met him. I told them that it was through a friend in another county who took me to Newport News to meet another guy who knew a bunch of dealers. The first dealer he introduced me to lived in a trailer park. I bought a sheet of acid (LSD) from him. That sheet sold in a hurry. I made five hundred dollars from a one hundred-dollar investment. The next time I went to him, I bought a half-pound of bud. When I went back there again, I found out that he'd just gotten busted.

With that source gone, I had to find a new one. That's when Shane, who said that he had gone to high school with me, introduced me to Clint. Shane told Clint that he had known me for a long time, and that I could be trusted.

At first, Clint was reluctant to sell me a pound or even a half. He told me that the most that he could ever sell me was a quarter pound because that's all that his connection could supply at one time. After several weeks of buying quarter pounds every single day, Clint finally gave me his telephone number and told me to call him the next day when I needed some more. This really impressed Shane, because all he'd ever had was Clint's pager number. Hell, he didn't even know where Clint lived.

The next day I called Clint and he gave me directions to his apartment. When I got there, he didn't have any bud, but he was waiting for his delivery. Pretty soon there was a knock at the door. It was Hank, Clint's "hook-up" with a plastic shopping bag in one hand and a cell phone in the other. He was clad in leather from head to toe and there was a chrome pistol in his waistband.

They went into Clint's bedroom. After Hank left, Clint invited me into the bedroom. He placed an empty dresser drawer on the bed and poured the contents of the shopping bag into it. There must have been twenty pounds there! It was in the form of "bricks", which we had to pull apart. That's when I realized that Clint could get me whatever quantity I needed.

After that, my business exploded here in the county and surrounding areas. I simply couldn't get the stuff fast enough. Not only was I supplying this county, but also a neighboring county and the city of Williamsburg, where I was legitimately employed.

When I met Annette, I had started to pay less attention to my business and more attention to her. My business was actually on a decline. I was down to getting five, or so, pounds a week for "D-Man" and a couple of quarter pounds, or so, for others. I was even supplying the parents of some of my friends!

When I got busted and went to jail, I decided that it really wasn't worth it and I didn't want anything else to do with it. But Sam kept on hounding me. At that point I was even getting upset, wondering how he was able to buy beer for us without getting into any kind of trouble because, as far as I knew, it was against the law, and cops aren't supposed to break the law.

That's when they told me that Sam's nickname was "Zero" and that the only thing he ever turned up, that was worthwhile, was me, and that he's only an informant, not a cop.

Chapter Eight

Internal Hell

The weight of all this was beginning to affect my very existence. I was actually becoming something that I had been taught to hate, ever since I was very young. My birth father, a drug dealer himself, always made it very clear that you *never* talk to cops and that, he felt, that narks are the lowest life form, next to "pigs" (cops), and that they don't deserve to live.

That night at Annette's, I was sitting on the kitchen floor. Annette was seated on a chair while Lora was brushing her hair. I was really in the pits. I was trying to explain to them, that even though I had only known Clint for a relatively short time, I felt that I just couldn't bring myself to set him up. Hell, I'd been seeing him and his girlfriend almost every day for nearly a year. During that time, his baby was born and we really did form a very close friendship. Lora, trying to reassure me, said that I shouldn't take it so personally, that it's not really my fault, that it's Clint's own fault since he, and not I, made the decision to do what he has done with his life. Still, I had a big problem with the whole thing and really didn't think that I could pull it off.

A few days later a new number appeared on my pager. The caller identified himself by the code, "50". When the number answered, the caller introduced himself as "Barney", one of the agents who was present at the firehouse the other night. He wanted me to arrange for a "controlled buy" of a pound of marijuana from Clint that night. I called Clint and made the arrangements. I called Barney back to confirm and he would pick me up later.

The stress of what I was about to do was unbearable so I started drinking beer. Before I knew it, I was hammered and the trashcan was full of empties. Meanwhile, Annette called. She knew instantly, from the tone of my voice and from my sloppy speech that my frame of mind was not good and she wanted me to stop over before I left for Newport News and to bring her some beer. I continued drinking until Barney came by to pick me up. I stuffed my backpack full of beer and headed out. I told Barney that I needed to stop by at Annette's for a moment. He was cool with that and away we went.

We rolled up in front of Annette's house. Barney waited in the car while I went inside. Shelly, Sam's daughter, was there visiting Annette. We quickly went up to Annette's room so that Lora wouldn't notice the backpack. That's when Annette noticed that I was wearing the "Grateful Dead" shirt that she had given me a month earlier. I told her: "Yeah, I thought it would be nice if I wore a little something from you, just in case ..." That's when she handed me a couple of tranquilizers. I popped them into my mouth and chased them down with a beer. Shelly had her own agenda. She pleaded with me, to get her a couple of ounces of coke while I was in Newport News. She even had the cash up front! I played it off, obviously she didn't know about my new association with the cops.

By now I was really wasted and it seemed like the trip to Hooters took forever. Five agents were waiting when we arrived. We picked a discreet parking spot at the far end of the lot where I was asked to step out of the car. Then they patted me down and handed me the transmitter, which was disguised as a pager. They insisted that I place it in the inside pocket of my jacket.

I got into the truck with Jerry and we drove across the street to Clint's apartment building. He handed me eleven hundred dollars and I went inside. Clint remarked that it had been a while since he had seen me. I told him that I was trying to lay low for a while until the heat died down from my recent bust. He handed me a beer and told me that the price would have to be a little higher than usual this time, since I hadn't been steady for a while. I handed him a grand and the deal was done. He figured that I was somewhat disappointed but said that my one hundred dollar profit for the night really wasn't too bad.

Back in the truck, I handed the bag to Jerry and, of course, he wanted to know how much it had cost. I told him and handed him the hundred. Then he said, out loud, "Deal done" and we drove back over to Hooters where I was patted down once more. As I chugged down the last swallow of my beer, one of the agents asked me if it was good. I told him that it wasn't the brand that I usually prefer, but that it was cold.

On the way home, we stopped at one of the agent's offices. There they all wanted to discuss every detail of what had just gone down. Several of the agents felt encouraged because, they believed, that they had "made" Clint's connection. They were a little put out by the fact that I would not let any of them go inside with me, but they played that off by claiming that I wasn't the only informant who they had dealing with Clint and that I probably wouldn't have to make any more buys from him anyway. Could it be, were they really through with me or was this just the beginning? The agent, nicknamed "Money", because he was always the one who paid me, handed me a slip of paper to sign and then he gave me back the hundred. Then they debated who should take me home and Money got the privilege.

On the way back, Annette paged me to call her house so Money let me use his car phone. Annette sounded really anxious for me to stop back in. Shelly was still there and they both sounded like they were feeling pretty good. They even said that they wanted to do a strip show for me. I shared these details with Money and he agreed to drop me off there. Before we could get there, Annette paged again. This time she was moaning and groaning and begging me to hurry.

Money dropped me off a short distance from Annette's house, as he didn't want his car to be seen there. Meanwhile, I waited for Annette to page me again, signaling that her mother had gone to sleep. It was around midnight in February and I was wearing my favorite "shredded" jeans. Those things had more skin than cloth and, after about forty-five minutes, I was getting really cold. I decided to peek into a window to see what was going on. I could see someone lying on the couch in the sunroom, but I couldn't make out who it was. I figure that it must be Lora, so I went around to the side of the house where a ladder was lying. I put it up to Annette's window. I went up and could see someone lying on Annette's bed and figured that they were probably both passed out. There was an air conditioner in the window but I managed to crack it open and squeeze my way in. I rolled onto the couch under the window and crept across the room to Annette's bed where I found Shelly sprawled out, passed out and naked. I saw no sign of Annette, so I decided to wake Shelly and find out where she is. I figured that she was probably somewhere downstairs, but I couldn't go down to look for her.

Shelly was no help. What little she said was unintelligible and she just kept dozing off so I decided to take a chance and went downstairs myself. I quietly slipped past the open door to Lora's bedroom and made my way to the sunroom at the front of the house. There I found Annette, asleep, curled up on the couch, wearing only a blouse, cradling her cordless phone in her arms. I took the phone from her hand and tried, quietly, to wake her. Eventually, she awakened enough to go upstairs.

Back in her room, she wanted to know if I was interested in having both her and Shelly. I told her no, because, after having watched many episodes of "Love Line", I knew pretty well that threesomes are usually destructive to monogamous relationships and that ours meant more to me than that. That having been said, we spent the night on her couch so as not to disturb Shelly.

Morning came quickly and I was dreading the long walk home, but I had to leave in a hurry, before Lora found out that I had spent the night. Annette found some warm clothes for me to put on and then she and Shelly both decided to walk with me. We snuck out of the back door.

I couldn't believe how much Annette cared about me. All my life, I've never been this close or this emotionally attached, to anyone.

When we arrived at home, my dad was still there, so I told them that they'd have to chill for a while until he went to work. I went inside and had breakfast and waited for my dad to leave.

After my dad left, the girls came inside and we partied. We raided his liquor cabinet and they got the bright idea to shoot pool, naked. I spent the entire time fulfilling Annete's every wish and she mine. I still wouldn't get next to Shelly, which obviously angered her. Later on, Annette and I showered together and this angered Shelly even more. At some point, Barney called, wanting to know if Annette was here with me because her mother had called him and told him that Annette was gone and had left a note, something about having to work out some problems. She figured that it probably had something to do with me, so she had Sam get a hold of Barney. I told him that I hadn't seen her. Finally, when Annette and I ended up in my bed, Shelly couldn't stand it any longer. After all, she wasn't getting much attention from either of us because we were totally into each other. So she decided that she wanted to call her dad to come and get her.

Annette was adamant that she didn't want to go home, especially with Sam there. She pleaded with Shelly not to call. Shelly didn't understand what Annette's problem was because there was a great deal more to the story than she knew. To prevent her from calling, I left one of the extensions off the hook. Shelly was picking up her clothes from all over the house, getting dressed. Then she busted into my room and called Annette every kind of slut. Annette jumped out of bed and responded in kind, then they came to blows and Annette ended up on a pile of clothes on the floor and Shelly stormed out of the house. Annette found a knot on her head and said that she needed another drink so I found a bottle of Crown Royal and brought it back to the bed. We polished it off and passed out in each other's arms.

The next thing I remember is when my dad was waking us up and a deputy sheriff was walking through our house. I learned later that Shelly had gone to someone's house and called her dad and told him that Annette was here. He told Annette's mom and she called the sheriff. The deputy and my dad both arrived at the house at the same time. My dad asked him what was up and the deputy told him that he believed that there was a fifteen year-old female runaway in the house. My dad couldn't believe it, so he invited the deputy inside to check it out.

At first, deputy Simpson said that, all he wanted, was to get Annette home to her mother. He closed my bedroom door and told us to get dressed. All the while she was dressing, she was saying how she really didn't want to go home. Finally deputy Simpson told her that this could be done the easy way, with her going willingly, or the hard way, with assistance. Finally, it became apparent that she would not go willingly, so Simpson called for a female deputy to respond to assist. Before the other deputy arrived, Simpson decided that Annette and I should be separated, as we were both really drunk and unreasonable. He wanted to usher Annette outside to wait in his car for the female officer. I decided to give him a hard time so my dad had to step in and restrain me while Simpson took Annette outside and handcuffed her to the pump at the well. In the process, Annette hit him several times.

When Capt. Hess arrived, she placed Annette in her vehicle and Simpson placed me in his. Unknown to him, I had a handcuff key attached to a cord around my ankle. My dad caught me trying to unlock my cuffs while Simpson was distracted by Annette. Then my dad took the key away, saying that escaping from custody would only make things worse.

I was really agitated by now and was ranting and raving to Simpson about how I was going to tell everyone who all of the task force agents and other informants are, and that this would blow all of their covers. I demanded that he let Annette and me go immediately. He was not impressed and carted me off to the Sheriff's office. On the way, Capt. Hess could be heard calling for backup, stating that Annette had managed to open the door to her squad car and was trying to get out of it at full speed. She actually had to pull over and restrain Annette until a unit with a cage divider arrived at her location.

Once at the sheriff's office, I was told that I was being charged with sexual battery of a minor. Deputy Simpson was sharing what I had said about the task force and they decided to call Barney and let him know what was going on. Meanwhile, Annette was in another room. She was giving Capt. Hess such a hard time, that they had to cuff her behind her back and shackle her ankles. They also had to connect the cuffs and the shackles with another pair of handcuffs. The captain then made her blow into a Breathalyzer and her blood alcohol level read at 0.35 percent. Hell, 0.08 percent is legally drunk in Virginia and people usually start passing out at 0.20 percent!

Barney arrived and explained his delicate position to Deputy Simpson and Capt. Hess and told them that he really didn't want to see this go any further. The problem now was, that my dad didn't really want me back home because, as he had explained to me a long time ago, I had now caused his house to be searched by the police because of something I had done. He told Barney, that if he wanted my help so badly, that *he* should find some place for me to stay, that I was just one big embarrassment to him and to his reputation in the community.

So there I was, abandoned once again, and the only one who really seemed to give a shit was Annette. Down the hall, I could hear her yelling how much she loved me, and sobbing.

One of the deputies was mocking her and this really pissed me off so I cussed him. My hands were still cuffed behind my back when this jerk tripped me up and slammed me down and I ended up with my face on the concrete floor with his knee on the back of my head. It was deputy Brooks, the same one who had busted me originally. Now he was busy writing me up for curse and abuse and being drunk in public. I tried to tell him that I would still be at home, not in "public", if Simpson hadn't dragged my ass down here.

Meanwhile, my dad was in with Annette and Capt. Hess. That's when Annette told my dad that Sam had taken her to Newport News with him on numerous occasions to purchase rock cocaine, which they would then smoke together. She told him that Sam would make advances toward her, touch her inappropriately and that he had even tried to "pimp her out" to some of his rock selling buddies there. She explained that this is why she didn't want to go home as long as he was involved with her mother. My dad then called Lora and told her what Annette had said. He could not believe her response. She said, yes, that Annette had told her these things also, but that it had been some time ago, and that Sam had promised her that it would never happen again! He told her that there would be a full investigation but that he would have to ask another locality to conduct it, since it would have been a conflict of interest for him to do so.

A mental health clinician was called in and it was decided that Annette was having suicidal ideation, so she was involuntarily committed for a psychiatric evaluation. My dad left to go home. Barney also left. I was taken to the jail, charged only with being drunk in public and curse and abuse, both of which are misdemeanors, and usually a person charged with these offenses is released "on his own recognizance" as long as someone over twenty-one will vouch for them.

By now the alcohol was wearing off and reality was beginning to return. I realized that I was on the way to losing what little was left in my life that had any meaning for me. I had already betrayed Clint, one of my most trusted friends, and my dad would probably never speak to me again. Not to mention Annette, how could we spend eternity together if I can't even stay out of jail? Just then, one of the guards, who remembered me from before, walked over and said: "I told you you'd be back." I told him that it was nothing I could help that they had come to my house and dragged me out of bed and that my dad had gone along with it. He asked me if there was anyone I could call to get me released. I told him that I'd pretty well blown it with my dad but he said that he'd known my dad for many years and that, deep down, I probably had a chance If only I could sincerely find the right words.

With a great deal of uncertainty, humility and shame I dialed the phone. My dad answered. He said that he'd been expecting me to call. I told him how ashamed I was about everything but that the internal hell I'd been going through was more than I could bare and, even though I knew it was wrong, how being in Annette's arms meant more to me than anything. I couldn't believe it when he said OK that he'd be down to get me in about half an hour.

I was worried to death about Annette, so as soon as we got home, I called her house. Sam answered. I could tell that he'd been drinking. He said' "Has that little girl been telling lies about me?" I told him that I didn't know what he was talking about and he said that Lora and Annette didn't come home and that he didn't know where they were. A few days later I learned that the task force agents had given Sam a urine test to see if he was really using crack and that a child protective services investigator from Gloucester County was trying to locate him. The urine test was positive for cocaine and Sam was nowhere to be found. I've never seen or heard from him again.

Chapter Nine

Too Close For Comfort

A few days later, I was at Annette's when I received a page from Barney. He had heard, from Sam, about a certain house in a local subdivision where, he believed, a lot of drug activity had been occurring, and that he knew that I was well connected to all of the people involved. He wanted me to do some controlled buys of marijuana there as well as buy some crack from a dude named Sammy. He wanted to know how much time it would take for me to set these up. I told him that it didn't really matter, that I could have it done just about any time, so he said that he would be back in touch later in the week.

At first, I had a really eerie feeling about this. It was one thing to set up Clint, who lived about fifty miles away, but now they wanted me to set up people who I'm around almost every day. I started to think about all of the people who had taken advantage of my trust in the past and then, when I ended up in jail needing money, nobody was there for me. There was Mac, who once owed me around four hundred dollars. About a year earlier, times were really hard, and I had given him the money to buy a quarter pound. Since that time, whenever I saw him, and asked him for the money, he always had an excuse or would just give me ten or twenty dollars or a couple of hits of acid or a small amount of bud. Finally I got fed up and demanded that he pay me. His excuse, once again, was that the money was all tied up in bud, so I told him to give me the bud in return but all he had was about an ounce and a half. Then there was Jimmie. Jimmie still owed me for the two ounces that I had fronted him the night before I got busted the first time. And then there was Sammy, who was responsible for getting Annette hooked on crack. Not to mention, back in high school, he once sold me fifty bogus hits of acid for a hundred and fifty dollars. Maybe Barney and the gang would be satisfied if I just delivered these three losers.

Barney called back in a few days and wanted me to make some buys with them that night. He wanted to know if I could go for some bud or some rock. I told him that it didn't matter to me, that I could get both, and we agreed to meet later that night.

As usual, I had to get my courage up and my conscience down, so I proceeded to get hammered with all of the beer I could get my hands on. This wasn't easy since my dad was right there at home, so I spent a lot of time out in our workshop until my pager went off. The display read, "50", which was the signal to stand by at the end of the driveway by the road. I couldn't believe my eyes. We live on a dead end road with hardly any traffic, and now, here come four vehicles, all at once. Jerry turned in to the driveway and the other three continued on to the end of the road, parking at the little public beach on the river there.

When I got into Jerry's truck, I told him that this "caravan approach" was much too obvious. After all, here we are in a very rural area where everyone knows what everyone else is driving, and a strange vehicle is usually looked upon with suspicion. Could he imagine what kind of suspicion four strange vehicles would arouse all at once?

We drove to the beach, where we met up with the other three cars. I was told to get out of the truck and, immediately, Barney patted me down, and then Money handed me the bogus pager. They were eager to get as much done on this evening as possible. They wanted the details of the arrangements I had made. I said, "I haven't made any, just give me a phone." They were incredulous. Barney, especially, seemed disappointed and, it seemed that he was rethinking whether he had done the right thing by getting those charges against me dropped. I reassured him that it was all good and, again, asked for the phone.

The cell phone wouldn't work at the beach because the area was so much lower than the surroundings, so we drove back up the road to a better spot. First I called Lana's house to see if Mac was there. Bill answered the phone, and when I told him that I wanted Mac, he thought that he knew exactly what I had on my mind. He said that Mac wasn't there but that what I was after was, and that it was cool to come right over. Next, I called Sammy's house and his brother, Clarence, answered. Yes, the same Clarence who had made my bail. He said that Sammy had gone out, but that he would contact him and would page me back when he had reached him.

The response came in less than a minute. It was the same number that I had just called. I called back and Clarence said that, if I could pick him up, he would take me to where Sammy was. Jerry nodded, "OK", and I told him that we were on our way. In a couple of minutes my pager went off again; it was Clarence's number, and we were nearly at his house, so we drove past it and called him. That's when Clarence told me that Sammy was at a nearby motel, throwing a party, and he gave me the room number and told me to just go there and see him. Coincidentally, the motel was located right beside a restaurant where I cooked on a part time basis at the time.

I told Jerry that I needed to stop in at the restaurant for a minute to pick up my paycheck. We did, and I went inside and got my check. Then we drove around the side and parked in front of Sammy's room. When I got inside there were only Sammy and one other guy there. They wanted to know who the dude in the truck was and if he was cool. I told them that his name is Jerry, a tugboat captain, and that he'd been hooking me up with bud for a while now. This seemed to satisfy them. Then he said that he didn't have the rock at the motel and that we'd have to go elsewhere to pick it up and he didn't have a ride. Jerry was happy to oblige.

Sammy and his friend got into the back seat of the truck. As we were leaving, several other cars arrived. Sammy shouted to one of the guys, that he'd be right back and that they could go ahead inside. A dude named Lamont, with whom I'd had several run-ins in the past, walked up and wanted to know who else was in the truck. This made me feel very uneasy since Lamont has hated my guts since high school. Sammy told him to chill out and then told Jerry to go on.

We ended up at a house about a mile from my home. The other guy went to the back door and Sammy went to the garden shed while Jerry handed me a one-hundred-dollar bill. I stepped outside and met Sammy on the back porch. He pulled out a plastic sandwich bag containing a number of twenty-dollar pieces of crack in smaller plastic baggies. He handed me five and I asked him to give me another, trying to impress upon him how desperately I needed this stuff. I gave him the hundred and he gave me six pieces of rock. He wanted to stay here for a while longer so he would not be returning with us. Back in the truck, I handed the buy to Jerry, who said out loud: "I have six twenty-pieces" and then he dictated all of the license numbers of the cars, which were parked in the driveway.

The next stop was the maintenance garage at the local office of the Virginia Department of Transportation (VDOT), the highway department, in Saluda where they patted me down and placed the evidence in the trunk of Barney's car. They wanted to know if Sammy had any more of the stuff and I told them, yes. Then they discussed the possibility of whether they had sufficient evidence to obtain a search warrant to search the house.

At this point, Barney reminded Money that, to protect themselves from liability in the event that something should ever happen to me due to my work with the task force, I needed to sign a liability waiver so that neither I nor my dad could sue the state, or the task force members, for damages. Since I couldn't read it due to my severe dyslexia, Money read the form to me. I signed it and he witnessed it. Although I've asked for a copy of this document several times and they've promised to give it to me, I have yet to get it.

Now it was time to go to Lana's. When we arrived, Jerry handed me four one-hundred-dollar bills. There was only one car in the driveway; it was Jimmie's. Jimmie met me at the door. Everyone else had left to go to a party and he had stayed behind to wait for me. He knew that I was coming and wanted to know what had taken so long. I told him that I had gotten caught up doing something and that I had stopped somewhere for a few beers. We went into the back bedroom where he produced four, one-ounce bags of marijuana. I told him that I wanted to buy it all. He said that, since the bud was not his, the price would have to be a hundred and twenty-five dollars per ounce. I told him that I didn't think that was fair, considering all of the bud I had sold to him in the past and had never tried to gouge *him* that way. He wouldn't back down. He kept saying that the stuff wasn't his and that he had to get something for his trouble. This made me feel even less guilty for setting him up and, anyway, he still owed me money from before. So I reached into my other pocket and pulled out another hundred dollars of my own, and the deal was done.

When I returned to the truck, I could hear Jerry saying Jimmie's license plate number out loud. I gave him the stuff and told him that he owed me an extra hundred because I had to spot it for him.

We drove back to VDOT and met up with the rest of the team. Barney, of course, patted me down right away, and Money gave me the hundred back and an extra two hundred and fifty for my trouble.

On the way home I asked Barney why they were spending all of this energy on these small-time dealers when they could be going after the really big ones in Newport News. He said that cleaning up our local community was more important to him than making big-time busts in Newport News. Suddenly, it occurred to me that, by "working" so close to home not only *my* life was being endangered, but Annette's as well. Why couldn't Barney see this also, or did he just not care?

The next morning, I awoke to the sound of my pager going off. It was Annette. She was calling to tell me that the house where I had gotten the crack from Sammy and the hotel room where Sammy's party was were both raided late last night. We both agreed that the proximity between my appearance there and the busts was bound to arouse people's suspicions.

A few days passed and I was sitting with Annette on her couch, drinking champagne, and I was wondering how things were going with Clint. By now I was wondering if, maybe, he'd been busted too. I called him up and his girlfriend answered. She was really glad to hear from me and had wondered where I had been. After all, I had helped them make quite a bit of money. I told her that I had been preoccupied with Annette and that she really didn't want me to take too many unnecessary chances. She seemed really happy for me and told me that Clint had just popped the question and had given her a four-carat diamond ring.

This was all I needed to hear. Just when these two think that all of their troubles are over, and their married life is all set to begin, somebody had to squeal on him and bring it all down. The only saving grace I could imagine was if Clint decided to "turn over" and turn state's evidence and help them get the goods on *his* connection, Hank.

The next time I heard from Barney, he wanted to know if I could set up another buy at Lana's house. I told him, no, because she was out of town so he asked if I could set up another crack buy with Sammy because they had come up empty when they raided the motel room and the house the other night. All they had gotten for their trouble was a few joints and some paraphernalia from some of the attendees. They still wanted to build a stronger case against him.

Feeling that I had no other choice, I agreed to set up a buy from Sammy. As usual, I got as drunk as I could before Jerry picked me up. To my surprise, the "team" consisted only of Jerry, Barney, and me. I had the distinct feeling that tonight's activity was strictly Barney's idea as no one else but Jerry was participating and he didn't seem to be too thrilled about it. Barney patted me down, as usual and handed me the "pager".

69

The receiver was in his car. I called Sammy's house and Clarence answered. He offered to take me to Sammy, but he wouldn't give out his location over the telephone. When we arrived at Clarence's, he motioned me inside and wanted to know how well I knew Jerry. I told him the same thing that I had told Sammy but he seemed to have his doubts. Not that he doubted me, but that he doubted Jerry. Anyway, he must not have had too strong a doubt because he ended up getting into the truck with us. As we were driving, he kept on looking back. Then something must have spooked him and he told Jerry to pull into a convenience store parking lot, Tall Chief Market. He waited until the car, which had been behind us, passed and then he must have felt reassured, because he wanted to continue on.

We turned onto another road and there was Barney, turning around in a driveway, and Clarence seemed to be suspecting that something was up, especially when the car pulled out behind us once again. We turned onto a gravel road but Barney kept going straight. We could see him turning around in the distance. At this point, Jerry acknowledged that he thought that something just wasn't right and that we should call it off. He kept saying out loud, "Yea, we'll just have to do it on another day." His voice got louder and louder as Barney's car got closer and closer. We reached the dead end of the road and, as we were turning around in a driveway, Barney drove up and turned his car around in the driveway right next door. Now Barney was ahead of us and Jerry hauled ass, as fast as he could, back to Clarence's house. We told Clarence that that could have been a close one and that we might do it some other time, but for tonight, we were going to Newport News, where we knew it was safe.

We headed back to VDOT to debrief. On the way I was really troubled, thinking about that waiver I had signed. Apparently Barney didn't care who got hurt as long as he got as many "busts" as possible to his credit, after all, he was trying very hard to enhance his image in the community, but tonight he had jeopardized two lives.

Back at VDOT, Jerry appeared concerned that the setup was flawed in that they didn't even have the full team and he vowed never to let Barney talk him in to a half-ass set up like this again. Jerry could see that I was pretty worried too, so he gave me fifty dollars for the night's work even though we didn't score.

Chapter Ten

Crashed

The next couple of weeks were quiet and I spent most of my time with Annette. Due to my learning disabilities, I qualified for help finding employment from the Department of Vocational Rehabilitation. I had lost my job at the four-star restaurant in Williamsburg when I got busted. Now my "Voc-Rehab" counselor wanted me to beg for my job back, but that's not my style, so, when she took me there I spoke to the head chef and told him that I was changing my ways. He called a couple of days later and, it was really no surprise when he said no, but he did send me a nice letter of recommendation.

After that, I applied at numerous other restaurants but without success. It seems that everyone had read about my troubles in the papers and besides, my driver's license was suspended for six months. Now my only source of income was derived from the controlled buys I was making for the task force. This was really compounding my troubles and I was seriously beginning to fear for my personal safety and that of Annette.

Inevitably, the telephone rang. It was Barney. He had a list of buys for me to make and would pick me up after supper. Actually, Jerry picked me up and we drove down to the beach at the end of our road where we were met by three additional units. Immediately, I was asked to get out of the truck and Barney patted me down. Then they wanted to know if I had set anything up. I told them no. Jerry reassured everyone that I could take care of everything on short notice and he handed me his cell phone. Of course, it wouldn't work at that location so we drove back up the road.

I called Sammy's house and Clarence answered. He said that Sammy wouldn't be around until much later but that, If I needed some rock, he could hook me up. I told him that I'd call him back as soon as I could get the money up, that way I could check with Barney and the gang to see if they were interested in doing business with a new player. While they thought it over, Jerry asked me to call over to Lana's house to see if Mac was there so that I could buy some bud from him. Whoever answered the phone said that Mac was busy right then, but to come on over and discuss my needs in person.

Our caravan pulled into the sub-division. The first car kept on going, past Lana's house. Jerry and I pulled into her already crowded driveway. The car with the radio receiver pulled over at the next road behind the house and the fourth car just kind of drove around in circles.

Bill must have seen us coming, as he opened the door and hollered at us to come in. Jerry and I eagerly complied. The front door enters directly into the living room. There were lots of people there and Will was seated at one end of the couch. He had broken open a "blunt" cigar and there was a nice little pile of "manicured" (the seeds and stems had been picked out) bud on the coffee table. Some of the people had beer and so I asked Lana if there was any more where that came from. She sent me to the fridge in the kitchen. Then I walked down the hall to go to the bathroom. While I was gone, everyone was talking to Jerry. They thought that, because he was with me, he was "cool". In fact, they thought that he was my new source and they were eager to try to get him to do some business with them. When I returned to the room, Jerry was explaining that he was only interested in a quarter pound to hold us over for the night, but that he

73

could arrange for as much as they wanted, later on when his boat would arrive. Will finished rolling the blunt, sparked it up and, after taking a good couple of "hits", passed it around the room. Lana told Jerry that she was on her way to Newport News to buy some bud and, if he wanted her to get some for him, he would have to front her the cash. With only slight hesitation, Jerry handed her four hundred dollars.

When the blunt got around to Jerry, he tried to play it off like he was too engrossed in his conversation with Lana to notice. When they persisted, he said that he wanted to stay straight until he could stay off the road for the night. Of course, when it was my turn, I had to make it look convincing.

Everyone thought that Jerry and I were a couple of "crackheads", so it was no surprise to anyone when Jerry asked Lana if I could use her phone to call Clarence. Clarence was ready to do business and Jerry told Lana that we would meet her later that night, when she got back from Newport News.

Outside, in his truck, Jerry asked me if the blunt had been any good. I told him that he was damned lucky that I'd taken a couple of hits from it because his refusal almost made us look suspicious.

Our caravan regrouped at the golf course and then it was on to Clarence's house. There is a small, country post office at the beginning of the road where Clarence lives. That's where three of our vehicles remained while Jerry and I went on to his house. Clarence invited me inside and then he had to make a quick phone call. He was calling his connection at Green Branch Mobile Home Park and making sure that nothing had changed.

Everything was cool so he came on outside and got into the truck with us. We drove to the trailer park, about two miles away. The other units kept well out of sight. When we arrived at our destination, Jerry handed Clarence eighty dollars in recently crumpled, brand-new twenty-dollar-bills. Clarence and I went inside. There were a couple of guys at the kitchen table where they had a block of rock cocaine roughly the size of a cigarette pack and probably valued between fifteen hundred and two thousand dollars. They were cutting off little pieces about the size of my little fingernail, which sell for twenty dollars each. Clifford told them that we wanted an "eightball" (eighty dollar piece), a chunk about the size of a sugar cube. The guy who cut the chunk said to Clarence, "That's 'phat' (a good value) for eighty dollars" and then he handed it to me.

Back in the truck, I handed it to Jerry and he produced a small electronic digital scale, about the size of a pocket calculator. He announced the weight out loud and then wrapped it in a cellophane cigarette wrapper. Clarence appeared a little anxious in the back seat as he didn't quite know what to make of this. I was kind of anxious myself.

Finally, we left the trailer park and returned Clarence home. Next we all met up at the VDOT shop to wait for Lana to return from Newport News. She was to meet Jerry and me at the Exxon station in Saluda.

By now, everyone was hungry so Money went to Hardee's™ and returned with a bunch of food and drinks. They all dug right in, but I couldn't eat a thing. I didn't want to lose what was left of the buzz that I'd gotten from drinking earlier and from the hits off the blunt at Lana's. Besides, the reality of what I was doing made me really nervous, my stomach was in knots.

Jerry wanted to know if I knew the guy who had sold me the rock or if I could identify him later on. Of course, I said no, because I didn't want to get in any deeper than I already was.

The time to meet Lana was fast approaching so we left. It wasn't long before she arrived with Jimmie in his red mustang cobra. She brought her backpack and jumped into the back seat of Jerry's truck. She didn't want to do the deal right there under the lights and in such a public place, so Jerry drove us to a nearby public boat landing at the end of a dead end road. Ironically, the sheriff's office and the regional jail are both located on this same road.

At the boat landing, Lana produced the quarter pound. I could see the excitement in her eyes as I vividly remembered the "rush" I used to get from dealing that amount of weight. Jerry had his little scale and he had to weigh the bud in smaller portions and then add it all up.

We took Lana back to where Jimmie was waiting and they left. We returned to the VDOT shop to debrief. I was telling them how badly it made me feel to see Lana set up like this. They tried to tell me that it really wasn't all that bad, that she'd probably "turn over" the way I did. All in all, though, I didn't see either alternative, going to jail or setting up your friends, as a very good idea.

Money paid me two hundred and fifty dollars but I was expecting three. He explained that he had to deduct fifty dollars for the "advance" that Jerry had given me previously when nothing went down. Barney was elected to drive me home because he is the only one who actually lives here in this county. The others are all from out of the area. On the way home, he told me that he thought that two hundred and fifty dollars was

76

pretty good money for one night's work and that I should feel lucky because he wished that he could make that kind of money. I guess that I was supposed to feel better about what I was doing, since I was getting paid, as if this money could make the guilt and shame go away. Hell, I used to make two grand a night before I started working with these guys.

Back at home, I called Annette and told her what I'd been up to. She told me about a party that was going on at a friend's house. His parents weren't home and practically everyone I knew would probably be there. That sounded cool, but I really just wanted to chill with Annette for a while. Anyway, she couldn't go to the party because her mom had grounded her for some reason. I would have snuck my car over there but my dad had taken the tags off of it the last time that I drove it drunk and with a suspended license. And tonight, at this late hour, he was in no mood to take me to her house.

I called over to the house where the party was. They put Stick Man on the phone. He had come all the way from Newport News! He said that he would give me a ride as long as I contributed to the beer supply. Of course, I said: "No problem."

The party was mobbed. I went to put the beer into the fridge, but it was already stuffed with brew.

Surrounded by all of my friends, the reality of my betrayal of them was hitting me with full force. All I wanted to do was to stop the horrible pain of this reality so, as usual, I tried to drink myself into oblivion. I couldn't stand it any longer, so I went into the kitchen and called Annette. I told her how I felt like pure shit and that I wished I were dead. I was even beginning to second guess my true motives because, I felt that wanting to be with Annette this much was, somehow, selfish since I was getting what I wanted at the expense of many of my friends.

Annette tried to reassure me that everything would turn out OK and for me not to do anything foolish. She reminded me that she believed that there was a higher purpose for me or, otherwise, I probably wouldn't be here now. She reminded me of how I had come close to dying when I crashed my Blazer into the corner of a brick building, drunk, at two o'clock in the morning at over seventy miles an hour, nearly a year ago. When I was found, two hours later, I thought that I was stuck in a ditch at a friend's house. They took me to the local hospital where it was found that I had a broken jaw and other internal injuries. They were not equipped to deal with the situation there, so they flew me to a major trauma center in Norfolk.

The helicopter ride is just a blur, as I was still too drunk to know the gravity of the situation, or to care. What I thought about most was that I had to be to work the next day. Had I known Annette then, I'm sure that all of my thoughts would have been of her.

I didn't realize that I had passed out until Bill came into the kitchen and was standing by the fridge. He told me that I'd been asleep on the floor for a couple of hours. Sure enough, I was lying there with the telephone receiver still clutched in my hand. I asked him to toss me a beer and then I hung up the phone.

The phone rang immediately. A hush fell over the entire house. Kyle, our host, was worried that it may be his parents calling and he did not want them to know about the party. It was Shelly. She said that she'd been trying to call here for hours and that she couldn't get through and that Annette was worried that something had happened to me or that I'd done something really stupid. So I called Annette immediately and reassured her that I was OK and apologized for getting her all upset.

When I hung up the phone, Will came into the kitchen with a blunt. By now it was around three o'clock in the morning. Kyle told us that we'd have to smoke it outside because he didn't want to take any chances that his parents might smell it.

We all went outside and shared the blunt. When we went back inside we drank more beer and watched a movie until we all passed out. Of course, my dreams were of Annette.

The next morning Kyle's twenty-two year old brother was just coming back from somewhere. He was impressed by the fact that I had been lying on the living room floor, passed out, with a half full bottle of beer in my hand, and I hadn't spilled a drop!

By this time everyone was coming around. It was time for breakfast, so I went to the fridge and got a beer. Stick seemed amazed by this and said: "Man, that's got to be rough on your stomach!" I just thought to myself, how I'd much rather be drunk than to have to face reality, sober.

Later on, Bill suggested that we all should try out Kyle's dirt bikes. Of course, we were all drunk and having a blast. Nobody wrecked and no one got hurt. As we put the bikes back into the shed, I thought about what a good time this was and how bad it really was, ratting out these kids. The party lasted three days.

Chapter Eleven

Sick Of It All

I could not rationalize what I was doing any longer. There were no longer reasons enough for ruining other people's lives and I just wanted it to end. Not to mention that, now, people were really beginning to suspect that I have something to do with all of the raids that had been occurring lately. It was just too much to be coincidental.

Annette and I started discussing options. We finally concluded that the only thing that made sense was for us to leave the area together. We decided to give the appearance that we had broken up so that, when the time came to leave, no one would suspect that we were together. Now, instead of calling her on the phone whenever I wanted to, I had to wait for Annette to page me, indicating that her mother was not around. Even when her mom was there and heard her talking to me on the phone, she would lie and tell her that she was talking to other guys. She even bad-mouthed me in front of her mom to make it look good.

My activities with the task force continued as usual. There were more controlled buys from Lana and Sammy and they finally got Mac to sell an ounce of bud to Jerry. This greatly increased Mac's confidence and there was talk of Jerry getting him five pounds. The price was negotiated and agreed upon: nine hundred dollars a pound. A date, several weeks away, was set for the transaction.

A few days later I was leaving Annette's house on foot when Mac drove by and picked me up. He was asking me if I believed that Jerry could really come up with that kind of weight. I told him that I thought that it wouldn't be a problem since he had sold me those kinds of quantities in the past. He gave me a beer and drove me home.

When the day for Mac's "big deal" finally arrived, he called me and, once again, told me how important this was to him and to me, if I knew what was good for me. After that, I no longer felt guilty for setting him up.

This was the same day that Annette and I had chosen for our getaway because, after this, everyone would surely know exactly what I had been up to. As that time neared, Annette discovered that she did not have anything that could qualify as luggage. She used this ruse over the phone, telling me to come and get all of the stuff that I had left at her house: shoes, clothes, etc. So I drove over to her house with no tags on my car and took her a duffel bag, which I had hidden in my back pack. I carried it inside and, since it seemed like such a long time since we had been together, we just wanted that moment to last and last and last. Her mother was at work and another lady was staying with her. We decided that it shouldn't look like we were leaving together, so we decided to meet at a nearby house in a few minutes.

Annette climbed into my car and we drove to my house. Finally, I had Annette back in my arms. We were both anxious and nervous about the plans that we were making, to turn our backs on everyone we knew and just get away and be together forever. She kept on telling me how much she loved me and wanted us to be together always. I had a fifth of vodka but she said that she didn't want anything to drink then, but that she'd probably need it later, so I gave it to her and drove her home, where I dropped her off at the same house where we had met earlier.

The time for Mac's big bust was nearing. I went back home and waited for my pager to go off, signaling that Jerry and the gang were coming for me. I did my usual romp in the woods with the dog and got as screwed up as I could.

Jerry came and we went to the VDOT shop where there were at least fifteen other agents waiting, many of whom I had never seen before. I became a little unsettled when one of them was telling another that his team nearly lost an informant the previous day when someone had shot at the informant's front door. Luckily the guy made it out of the back door alive.

Now it was time for the pre-game planning session. Jerry repeated several times, the key phrase: "We're gonna treat you right", which was the signal for when the bust was going to go down, in other words, for when the rest of them should storm the place. Other arrangements included calling another locality to borrow a drug-sniffing dog for the occasion and, locally, the use of two uniformed officers to take any prisoners to jail.

The location for the deal was to be the same Exxon station in Saluda where we had picked up Lana previously to buy the quarter pound, only this time we were operating in broad daylight.

When we arrived at the Exxon station we expected to find Mac and his red Firebird. Instead, There was Lana and Jimmie's younger brother, Aaron, in her little Escort. We pulled around near the back and they joined us there. On Jerry's suggestion, I got out of the truck and got into the back seat, allowing Lana to get in front with him.

She handed forty-five hundred dollars to Jerry and he handed her a five-pound brick of bud, about the size of a breadbox, wrapped in Saran Wrap.

Next, Jerry produced a smaller, two-pound brick and asked Lana if she thought that she could get rid of that also. If so, he offered to "front" this to her, saying that she could pay him some time next week. This must have appealed to her since she said "yea" without any hesitation whatsoever. Then they shook on the deal as Jerry was saying the magic words: "We'll take good care of you."

Lana exited the truck and I moved back into the front seat. Before I could close my door completely, there were agents surrounding both vehicles. They were all in plain clothes and were wearing their badges on neck chains that were now exposed. They shouted that they were state police officers and they had their guns drawn. At least two agents took control of each of us, including Jerry, and walked us to the back of our respective vehicles. I gave my guys a bunch of shit to make it look good. Aaron picked up on my apparent righteous indignation and responded likewise.

Just then, the drug-sniffing dog arrived in an unmarked car with official tags, accompanied by a uniformed handler. At this point, there was only "suspicion", no one had yet been placed under arrest. Now the dog handler put the dog to work. First he took the dog to Jerry's Blazer. The dog circled it a couple of times and also went inside. He seemed to detect some indication of marijuana but there was no physical evidence to be had. Lana's car was next. As soon as the door was opened, the dog went off and the seven pounds were discovered. Instantaneously and simultaneously we were all handcuffed and read our rights. Then we were all separated and carefully patted down. When Barney searched me, he found some cash in my pocket, which he loudly confiscated, in keeping with the spirit of the occasion. He then sneaked it back into my pocket with a wink.

Just then, the marked patrol cars with the uniformed officers arrived. Jerry and I were placed in one car, he in the front and I in the back. We all ended up in the prisoner receiving area at the jail. Jerry, Aaron and I were placed in the only holding cell together and Lana was handcuffed to a stationary bench. We had arrived just in time for dinner (fake chicken patties). I told them all that they'd better eat up because it would be a long time until breakfast.

Jerry was the first to get to go into the conference room to see the magistrate about his "bail". After a few minutes, he was released "on his own recognizance". Next came my turn and, amazingly, I got the same deal. The VDOT shop was within walking distance and they told me to go there and to meet Jerry.

As I was walking along, I realized that my life, as I had known it, was now surely over and that I just had to get away.

Jerry and most of the other agents, except for Barney and Money were waiting at VDOT when I walked up. We had to wait a while for them. While we were waiting, one of the agents asked Jerry if he would take me back to the trailer at Green Branch to make another rock buy. I told them that I thought that that was a really stupid idea because, by now, surely everyone must know that I'm a nark and that they'd probably try to kill me if I showed up anywhere else. Then somebody made a stupid comment, something about how they could get an attempted murder charge for someone and then somebody else quipped back: "We could hold him still and get the full charge."

Finally, Money and Barney returned and now it was time for *my* payoff. Four hundred dollars and a ride home.

Chapter 12

On The Run

As soon as I got home I had to call Annette. I needed to reassure her that everything had gone OK. She must have been worried because, she said, she had tried to reach Sammy to get some crack to ease her anxiety, but he never returned any of her pages. We talked for more than an hour, planning our escape. The whole time that I was on the phone with her, I was packing everything we would need for our trip. We didn't have a clue where we were going, we just knew that we had to go.

An important part of our plan was to persuade everyone that I no longer had my car, that I had sold it. Even Jerry and Barney believed this, or so I thought. I had it stashed behind the house the last time that Barney brought me home. I had found where my dad had hidden the tags some time ago, and tonight I put them back on. He wondered why the car was behind the house. I just said that I wanted to keep it out of sight until I could drive again.

Secretly, I carried my belongings out of the back door and past the deck, into the car. I was really prepared for a long trip away. I had packed a small tent, sleeping bags, cooking utensils, a small camp stove, dishes and canned goods. My dad and I used to do a lot of camping when I was younger, and I really felt well prepared. I didn't want him to become suspicious, so I told Annette that I had to get off the phone and to page me when her mom was asleep. My dad didn't have a clue that I was packing the car the whole time I was on the phone, he was dozing in front of the TV in the living room while I was carrying everything out of the back door. I even had four half-gallons of vodka, which I had been saving for a special occasion.

My dad and I talked for a while until the eleven o'clock news came on. It was a sure bet that he would doze off again before it was over. Sure enough, by eleven-twenty he was fast asleep. Annette should have paged me by now. Could something have gone wrong? I couldn't stand it any longer so disconnected the receiver to the motion alarm, which guards our driveway, and snuck out of the back door and pushed the car into the front yard and as far down the driveway as I could before starting the engine.

I drove past Annette's house twice but everything was dark and she still hadn't paged me. I thought that, perhaps, she'd had second thoughts about our plan or that, maybe, her mom had caught on. I was definitely leaving now but I just couldn't leave without Annette, so I decided to go back home and think things over. My dad woke up when I got there. He wanted to know where I'd been and what I was doing driving again. I explained that I had been planning to leave but that, after thinking it over, I really had no place to go and that I might as well just stay and face the music. My dad thought that, at last, I was getting some sense, although he understood where I was coming from about leaving it all behind. He said that he, too, had had times in his life when he just wanted to have a fresh start.

Just when everything seemed like it might be OK, the dog began barking furiously. It was that special bark that he does whenever someone who doesn't belong here is approaching. A car was pulling away near the end of our driveway when we went outside to investigate. Then, in the shadows, I saw Annette standing there, she was in tears. My dad wanted to know what was going on and I told him that I really didn't know but that I would find out. He went back inside. Annette was crying because she had thought that I had left without her. She said that she had tried to page me several times but that, for some reason, it was not working. She had seen me the second time that I had driven past her house and she even climbed out of her window to meet me, but I was gone. My dad came back outside and told Annette that it was way too late for her to be out like this and that either he would take her home or call her mother to come and get her. Annette said no and ran out of the driveway. I headed toward my car and my dad said that, if that car leaves the driveway again, I could never return. I told him that I was sorry that he felt that way, but that I really believed I had no other choice. I knew that Annette would go straight to Sammy's if I didn't pick her up and she sure as hell didn't want her mom involved right now. So I jumped into my car and picked Annette up on the road. She showed me where her bag was stashed and we picked it up and were finally on our way.

We left Middlesex County by the fastest possible route without going on very many main roads. In about twenty minutes we were in another county and filled up the gas tank. Nervously I paid the cashier and we were back on the road. Now, we decided that it would be best to just stick to the posted speed limits, as we did not want to attract any unwanted attention. About fifteen minutes later my pager started going off. It was Barney's number. We stopped at a pay phone and I called my dad to see what he had said. He said that he had called the sheriff's office as soon as I pulled out of the driveway and that he'd told them that Annette was probably with me but he still didn't know that we were leaving the area, he just thought that we were spending the night somewhere. I felt reassured that our plan was still cool.

We drove the rest of the night, until dawn. I was taking any road that headed west, but had no clue where we would eventually end up. We just wanted to go where no one expected us to go and where no one could possibly recognize us. We were pretty confident, after all, we had planned this very carefully and felt that we were really well prepared. We had everything we needed and I had about six hundred dollars in cash.

When the sun came up we were still somewhere in Virginia on a deserted two-lane highway. We pulled in to a little town on a lake. It had a Dollar General Store™, a grocery store, a McDonald's™ and a hotel. The hotel overlooked the lake. In the parking lot there were lots of pick-ups with boat trailers. After driving all night I was really tired and grouchy. We were planning to look for a campground to save money, but by now the hotel seemed awfully inviting, so we decided to take a room. The manager had long ago seen her best days, she had one of those wilted blue beehive hair-dos. She asked me all sorts of questions. She wanted to know where I was from, my mailing address and my social security number. She wanted to know if we were on our honeymoon because, she said, she had some better rooms overlooking the water. The difference in price was only fifteen dollars, so I said sure. I paid in advance and she gave me the key. When we got up to the room, we took off our clothes and crashed.

When we woke up, some time that afternoon, we decided that we should do something to change our appearances, so we decided to go to the store to buy some hair coloring. We picked a box of blonde and a box of black.

Back at the hotel we decided that cutting our hair was also a good idea. I cut Annette's as well as my own. Since her hair is naturally auburn, she opted for blonde, and since I'm blonde already, I opted for black. We showered together and then she applied the coloring. The process really did a number on the hotel's towels. After we dried our hair, we got dressed and picked up some food at the McDonald's™ drive-through across the street.

After dinner we talked for a while. I was really wigging out because I thought that I had really blown it with my dad and that I'd probably never see him again, at least not on any sort of friendly terms. Annette continued to reassure me, saying that I'm not the only one who has been disowned by my family. It didn't seem to help much, though, because I was now realizing how much my relationship with my dad really meant to me and I was sure that her mom and grandma would never really turn their backs on her. Anyway, none of that really seemed important as long as we had each other.

I had brought along a road atlas and now we decided to plan our route. We figured that it would be better to drive during the daytime, especially if we were going to be on an Interstate, that way there was less chance of being recognized among the thousands of other cars.

The next day we left early and drove for about twelve hours. We pulled off the Interstate, somewhere in Alabama, and ended up on a two-lane highway at an intersection where there was a three-story hotel with a pool and a gas station. By now I felt more confident about using a fake social security number and address. The clerk asked me how many guests were in my party and I told her that I was by myself. We parked around back where the room was and carried our essential belongings inside. We decided that we would save money by eating some of the food that we had brought along from home, so we ate "Oodles of Noodles™" with canned chicken chunks, which we cooked on our "Hobo Stove" on the coffee table.

After dinner we decided that it had been way too long since we had been impaired, so we went across the street to the gas station to see what they had that we could mix with vodka. There was a lemon "Slushee" machine, so we bought four or five and took them back to our room. Back at the hotel we got enough ice to fill the bathroom sink and placed the Slushees in there. We poured vodka into the complimentary hotel cups and added the frozen lemonade. After that, I consumed about a quart of vodka while we took a shower and then we went skinny dipping in the hotel pool. By now we were thoroughly slammed. This was the first time that I'd ever made love in a pool. It was totally awesome but I still had enough energy for a repeat performance when we returned to our room.

Morning came way too soon and, of course, we had to have a shower before we hit the road again. As we were packing the car, I noticed that the muffler was hanging really low, so I liberated one of those steel coat hangers from the clothes rack in our room, the kind that has a ring on top to prevent it's removal. It really wasn't that hard to pry it off, but it was much harder fastening it to the car. I also wrapped some duct tape around where the muffler pipe had broken but the stuff really isn't very heat proof because, four hours later, the muffler was roaring again. It felt so blissful, just Annette and I and the open road ahead. The whole time that I was driving, I held Annette's hand in mine.

That afternoon (I'm not really sure where we were) I tried to call my dad from a pay phone at a gas station. He wasn't home, so I left him a message on our machine. I just told him that we were OK and that I'd be in touch.

Later on we had lunch at a Taco Bell™ somewhere off of Interstate 10 in Louisiana. Finally, the weather was warm enough so that we could remove the "T-tops" from the car. When we got back on the road, Annette was checking the atlas to find a location with a campground where we could spend the night. She found a spot on Route 1, right on the Gulf of Mexico and that became our destination for the day. We turned off of the Interstate onto a two-lane road with canals on both sides. At some point Annette noticed something in the water in the canal on the right. I pulled the car over to have a closer look. We got out and Annette, much to her delight, saw a small alligator there. She was just like a kid at the zoo who had just seen her first 'gator!

Around dusk, we finally arrived at the little town we had seen on the map earlier. It was nothing but a bunch of run-down buildings and trailers, right on the gulf. I asked about the campground at the store. The clerk said I was in luck, that they are the ones who operate the campground. She said that, if I wanted to rent a campsite, I would have to show her a picture ID containing my name and social security number. All I had was my restricted Virginia driver's license, which consisted of a green piece of paper. Reluctantly I handed it to her. She smiled and said, in that Cajun accent: "Honey, you ain't gotta worry about it, I ain't the law." So I paid her fifteen dollars and she gave me directions to the site.

-When we finally arrived we couldn't believe what we saw. There were no other campers there, just us. The campground consisted of a paved slab (for parking?) and a "pavilion" that had a one-stall toilet and a shower stall that the door was rusting away from. On the outside of the building there was a three-compartment sink. I'm not sure if the toiled flushed or if there was water in the shower or the sinks but we didn't stay around to find out. We returned to the store to get our money back. The lady at the counter said that they didn't usually give refunds. An older, and presumably much wiser, lady in the back shouted out: "What's wrong with it?" I told them that nothing was wrong with it, that it just wasn't what Annette had expected.

We got our money back and decided that, as long as we were here, it might be nice to sit on the beach for a while. We parked the car and sat on the hood for twenty or thirty minutes but the wind was so strong that sand kept blowing into our faces. This really wasn't the relaxing moment we had hoped for. As we were trying to pull back onto the highway, we realized that the car wasn't moving, we were stuck in sand up to the floor. Even the muffler was buried. Soon an old man who lived in a house nearby noticed us. He got some younger guys to come over and help push us out. It was apparent that they'd all been drinking but they were really friendly. I had to remain in the car because Annette didn't know how to work the clutch, so I felt kind of self-conscious just sitting there while everyone else was putting their backs into it.

Now that our plans for the night had fallen apart, we decided just to drive on until something else came along. The road that we were on was a deserted, endless road that followed along the gulf. The only thing we saw the entire time was an oilrig in the distance. As we were approaching a bridge that crosses over Lake Charles, we could see lots of blue police lights ahead and traffic was backed up at least a mile in all directions. We decided to pull into a convenience store. We asked the clerk if she knew what was going on up ahead, but she didn't. Another customer volunteered that the tie-up was due to an Easter celebration held at a nearby park, which was now just letting out, so we filled up the tank and decided that it was probably safe to proceed since everyone was looking to get home as soon as possible rather than to hold up traffic.

Eventually we made it to Houston. By now we were both really tired, especially me, since I had been driving for nearly fourteen hours and I was beginning to nod off at the wheel. Finally, around eleven-thirty, we spotted a hotel up ahead. By now we were starting to run low on money and were down to only forty or fifty dollars. This time check-in was a breeze. All the clerk wanted to know was my license plate number, which I gave her. When we got to our room we set up the hobo stove and cooked some more "Oodles of Noodles™". As soon as we finished eating, we both passed out in each other's arms.

The following morning while we were showering, I knew that something was definitely wrong. I felt like shit. My stomach was queasy and the skin on my face and on my head, especially where I had shaved it earlier, was on fire. I looked into the mirror and noticed that my face and head were blistering. Apparently I had gotten really sunburned from driving without the "T-tops" in place. I decided to take a couple of muscle relaxants to see if that would help. I've always kept some on hand, ever since I wrecked my Blazer that time, because I have painful muscle spasms in my back. Annette did not think that it was a good idea, but I took them anyway.

Realizing that we couldn't last much longer on the limited amount of money we had left, we decided that, perhaps, we could pawn some of our belongings. We gathered up cassette tapes, Annette's "Grateful Dead" ring, a really neat billy-club of my dad's, an old bayonet that he'd given me and my pager and went to the pawn-shop, which was right next door. The clerk wasn't interested in any of these treasures except for my pager but she said I still needed a photo ID if I wanted to do business. I tried to explain to her that my wallet had been stolen and that I didn't have a photo ID. She referred us to a second-hand store down the street.

We went to the place. The proprietor was a rotund older gentleman with a white beard. Before I even showed him what I had to sell, I explained about my stolen wallet and how I had no ID. He said, "No problem, let me see what you've got", so I showed him the stuff. He seemed interested in everything but the pager and offered me sixty dollars. He said that he was really sorry about my misfortune and then he asked to see the registration for my car, just so that he would have some information in case the police came looking for the stuff.

Solvent again, we went on our way. After about an hour, we stopped at another Taco Bell™ for lunch. While we were there, we stocked up on mayonnaise and taco sauce, just like we had stocked up on soap, shampoo and towels at the hotels.

About an hour after we were back on the road, we saw a sign directing us to a campground and several restaurants. We followed the signs to the campground. Once there, I asked how much it would cost to stay there for the night as well as the entire week. The night rate was fifteen dollars and the week was seventy-five. We drove around the place and it seemed pretty much on the up and up. Good toilet facilities and showers and even a laundry room. Then we drove around the local area, visiting every restaurant we could find, and put in employment applications. We asked lots of people where we might get hired and it sounded pretty promising so we decided to register for a week at the campground. It took almost all of the money we had left because we used the rest for gas and food.

That night we had grilled chicken breast, which I had bought at the grocery store, and rice. After dinner we pitched our tent and then we walked to the pond at the campground and started drinking vodka mixed with "Sunny Delight™". At the pond we reflected on our situation and were thinking how lucky we were to have each other. We wondered what was happening back home. Has anyone else gotten busted lately? And we were wondering how seriously the effort to find us really was. Of course, we also wondered what would happen to us next.

We were feeling pretty good when we crawled into our sleeping bags, which we had zipped together into one "double-bed" sized bag.

The next morning we went out and followed-up on the applications that we had turned in the day before. When we got to Frank's Truckstop, the lady told Annette that, indeed, they had openings for a cook and a waitress, but that Frank needed to speak with us in person before a decision could be made and right now wasn't a good time. So we went to McDonald's™ and ate lunch.

Back at the campground the owner wanted to know how our job-search was going. We told her about the possibility at Frank's and she was pleased. She said that Frank and his wife attended her church.

Later we went back and met Frank. He wanted to know about my cooking experience and how long we were planning to be in the area. At the same time, Annette was telling him how much she really liked the area and how she'd like to stay here for a long time. This seemed to be just what Frank wanted to hear. Then he introduced us to his son, a man in his thirties, who had us fill out the usual tax forms and so on.

I was twenty and Annette was fifteen. I gave my age as twenty-one and Annette gave hers as eighteen. Annette was scheduled to begin in two days and I was to start in four.

On the way back to the campground we bought some more chicken and hair coloring. The blonde rinse had turned Annette's hair more of a lighter shade of red, so she wanted black.

After dinner we went to a convenience store and bought a three-liter bottle of some kind of store-brand cherry soda for ninety-nine cents. It tasted sort of like bubble gum.

Back at the campground we put the soda into our cooler to chill. We drank vodka from a bottle, then we would pour the soda into a cup of ice and drink it as a chaser. We were sitting in the car at our campsite, listening to the radio and drinking, when Annette got the bright idea that it was about time she learned how to drive a manual transmission. I figured that it wouldn't do any harm if she just drove around in the campground. After a couple of close calls where she almost ran into stuff, I decided that it wasn't such a good idea, so we returned to the campsite.

I stuck a cassette tape into the car's radio and Annette immediately removed it because she didn't want to hear it, so I took the tape and broke it in half and threw it onto the floor and said, "There, now you don't have to worry about it." Her response was to get out of the car, go into the tent and take the vodka with her. Then, as I had done many times before when I had been angry with my dad, I started the engine and took off.

I drove to Interstate 10, about a block from the campground, got on and hauled ass to the next interchange. By then, I had cooled off enough to return to the campground. When I got back, the maintenance man bitched at me for spinning gravel when I left. Later I learned that Annette had been talking to him and had told him that I had left her stranded and that she was pregnant with my child, none of which was true. I asked her why she would make up such a tale, and she said that it must have been wishful thinking, at least the part about being pregnant. This was followed by a long discussion about her wanting a baby and my position that we shouldn't consider it until we were financially established. Her rationale was that, considering how far we had already come, after all we already both had jobs, by the time nine months were up, we would surely be in appropriate circumstances. But she didn't want to get pregnant on that particular night because, she thought that she was too drunk. Upon thinking about it some more, it occurred to me that, with a child, I would finally have that "whole" family that I've always wanted to be a part of. I was also kind of looking forward to being able to raise a child without making all of the mistakes that were made in raising me.

The following morning Annette dyed her hair black, then she went to Frank's to pick up her waitress uniform to wear to work that night. Some of the other waitresses, who had seen her on the previous day, made the remark to her, that they knew all the time that her hair couldn't possibly have been "that beautiful strawberry blonde" for real.

That night, when Annette returned from work, she said that she now wanted to get pregnant, so we spent the rest of the night trying.

On my first day at the job at Frank's, his son introduced me to everyone saying, "At last, we have a real cook." This made me a little apprehensive because I didn't want

98

to have a reputation that I couldn't live up to. Another cook, Alfred, said that he'd heard that I was looking for a place to rent and that he knew of an apartment that was available. I told him that I was definitely interested, so he called the owner for me. The owner came by to the restaurant to talk with me. He said that he needed to clean the place up a bit but, by the following night, it would be ready to move in.

Later that evening another cook, Ryan, offered for Annette and me to stay with him until we could do something more permanent. I was happy to accept this generous offer as I was getting pretty tired of living in a tent.

That night, at Ryan's house, he made a remark about how much alike Annette and I are, referring to our drinking. I asked him to join us but he declined, saying that his stomach couldn't handle liquor. We spent the night between our sleeping bags, hers underneath and mine on top, on the floor of his guestroom, as there was no bed.

Chapter Thirteen

A Home At Last

Around nine o'clock the next morning, Ryan was knocking at the door saying that he had to go to work. He told us that we could stay as long as we liked, just to lock the door when we left.

Instead of using Ryan's facilities, we went back to the campground and showered.

Annette was scheduled to waitress for lunch and I was off. The guy who owned the apartment came by after Annette's shift and took us to see it. It was upstairs in an old, dilapidated house that had been converted into three apartments, two downstairs and one upstairs. Ours was, supposedly, "semi-furnished."

We reached the top of the stairs and opened the door of the three-room apartment. We entered and found ourselves in the living room. It was bare except for the blue wall-to-wall carpeting. I noticed a door on the opposite, outside, wall and asked where it led. The guy said that there is a small veranda out there but that he wouldn't advise anyone going out there because it might be unsafe. To the left was the kitchen. It was "furnished" with a kitchen table and two plastic lawn chairs and had a refrigerator and a stove. The cabinets and the refrigerator had been spray-painted black and white.

Back through the living room to the bedroom. The bed consisted of a box spring and mattress on the floor. The mirrored headboard was at the head of the "bed", resting on two cinderblocks. There was also a vintage 1950's clock radio for our entertainment pleasure. The bathroom, which was just off the bedroom, had all of the usual appointments but no means to take a shower, only an old claw-foot bathtub.

Annette and I looked at each other and were thinking each other's thoughts: "What a dump". However, since we didn't have any other offers at the time, and the guy didn't even ask for a security deposit or for a month's rent in advance, we decided to take it.

We returned to the campground, took down the tent and gave the cooler back to the preacher who had loaned it to us and said our good-byes. Now we had a home, at last.

Later that night, lying in each other's arms, we reflected on what had transpired so far. We now believed that we had a good chance at pulling this off, but at the same time we worried about what might happen if we were caught. Certainly we would be separated, and for a long time, at least for two years, until Annette turned eighteen, May 7, 2000. This is when Annette revealed her reason for wanting to have a baby. She said that, even if we had to live apart for whatever length of time, with a baby, she would always have a part of me by her side.

The next day, Annette worked the lunch shift and I was off. I unpacked the car and set up the apartment. When it came time for Annette to get off, I went to pick her up. That's when Annette told me that the other waitresses had something for us. The manager at Frank's, Peggy, had something she wanted us to see. She walked us over to her pick-up, which was filled with all sorts of household supplies: dish drainer, silverware tray, dish towels, silverware, bath towels and soap, sheets, pots and pans, dishes, Tupperware™, cleaning supplies and much more. Annette was really excited but I didn't think too much of it since I've never liked taking charity. There were so many bags that Annette had to get into the car first and I had to pile stuff in her lap in order to make it all fit.

When we got back to the apartment we put everything away. Then we decided to shop for dinner. We bought five pounds of hamburger, some chicken breasts and some frozen orange juice concentrate (for screwdrivers). On the way back, we stopped at a drugstore and Annette bought a do-it-yourself pregnancy test.

Back at the apartment, I turned the hamburger into patties, which I then froze for use later on. Annette went into the bathroom to use the pregnancy test. She wouldn't let me in because she wanted to be the first one to see the results. When it was time to check the results, she went back in. She quickly came back out, all upset; the test was negative. I tried to reassure her that the test was not one hundred percent accurate, that her pregnancy might be too "new" to register on the test and that she should test again in a couple of days. So we started drinking screwdrivers and I cooked dinner.

After dinner we went downstairs to another tenant's apartment, Luke. We wanted some beer but didn't have the necessary credentials to purchase it. So we asked Luke if he would go to the store for us. I told him that I had lost my ID. He invited us in and said, "Sure". That's when I learned that his driver's license was suspended for driving under the influence of alcohol, so I drove him to the store. It was pretty crowded in the front of my two-seater sports car. He sat in the passenger seat and Annette sat on the center console with her legs next to his. She was wearing only a bikini bathing suit and he was really looking her over. I didn't worry, though, he was just a skinny, toothless old alkie, glad to have a ride to the store.

Later on, Luke and Ryan and some other folks dropped in to wish us well. There was plenty of beer and liquor and a little bit of pot and we had a good time. After all, it was better than living in a tent. After everyone had left, only Luke remained. We were on the veranda when Annette went inside to get a drink. Luke still couldn't take his eyes off her, he said: "Too bad you're not single." Annette just gave me a look that I could read, as if to say: "Don't get mad, just ignore it." Luke sensed the tension in the air and said that he meant no harm, it was just that Annette "really looked tight."

The next day we were scheduled to work the evening shift together. One of the other cooks, "Turtle", said that there's usually a party at his house after work and that we were welcome to stop by. At the end of the shift he gave me directions to his place. Annette wanted to go, but only to find someone of legal age who would help us to buy some beer.

I found the house and scoped out the neighborhood, making sure that I knew how to get home without having to take any major highways. There were cars parked all over the front yard. We went inside. The place was packed and they were running low on beer. Turtle took up a collection and I offered to drive the guy with the money to the store.

Back at the party, Annette and I each got a beer and sat down on the couch. She wanted to know if I had gotten the guy to buy any beer for us. I told her, no, that I would have been embarrassed to buy a case of beer and then go to a party and leave it in the car while we were drinking someone else's.

Annette really didn't want to stay. She kept bugging me to go home. Then someone rolled a blunt and I waited for my turn. All the while, Annette was whining to leave, even some of the other people at the party noticed. So, right after I took my hit off the blunt, I apologized to everyone for leaving so soon, and we got ready to leave. Annette had just gone out of the door when Turtle came up to me and said that we were welcome any time but that, if I ever wanted to stop by alone, that was OK too.

In the car, Annette explained that she had been uncomfortable inside because she didn't know anyone there and she couldn't understand how I could have been so comfortable among all of those strangers. I tried to explain to her, that I was used to this sort of thing, from all of the dealing that I had done, and that this was no different.

The next morning I awoke to the sound of a freight train passing by. Annette was already up. She had gone downstairs to borrow some orange juice for a morning cocktail. When she returned, we made our breakfast cocktails and then she began to tease me until I couldn't stand it any longer. We made love for the next hour.

After that, we discussed our options for trying to get some beer. Annette said that she had gotten to know this older guy, Fred, who washed dishes at Franks. He lived at the campground where we had stayed. We drove to the campground and paid him a visit. Fred said that he'd be glad to oblige but that he was getting ready for work and that he still had to take a shower. I told him that I'd be back in a few minutes. We went back home and changed into our work clothes. Then, while Annette stayed behind, I went back over to Fred's.

Fred was waiting for me when I arrived. We went to the grocery store and picked up four cases of long necks and a case of cans. As we were loading our purchase into the car, the preacher drove by and stared. I took Fred back to the campground and offered to pay him for his kindness but he would not accept it. I told him that I had to run home to put the beer on ice before I went to work. He said that I should stop back by on my way to work.

I got the beer home and it filled up the entire refrigerator, from top to bottom. This made Annette very happy. I had to be at work at three but Annette didn't have to be there until four.

I left for work and went back over to Fred's place. He invited me in and wanted to know if I was in a big hurry to get to work. I told him: "Not really." He handed me a forty-ounce bottle of malt liquor and we sat there and talked for a while. When we finally went to work we had a nice "buzz" going. When we got there, it wasn't long before Fred told Ryan and everyone how much beer I had bought. They all wanted to know what time the party was starting. I told them to just drop on by after work.

When I ran home to pick up Annette for her shift, she was drinking a beer. I asked her how many she had had and she said, "a few." I looked in the trashcan and there were three empties in there, so I grabbed one too. While she finished hers, I chugged mine. I asked her if she felt OK to go to work. She said, "sure", but I had my doubts. Unlike me, who was accustomed to working in an impaired state, Annette was not, but I took her anyway.

It wasn't long after we arrived back at work, when Annette came running into the kitchen and told me that she had just spilled iced tea on a customer. She was getting towels to soak it up and all of us back there were thinking how it must suck to be her right now. Frank's wife asked her what was wrong and Annette told her that she was suffering from "morning sickness", so she told her that she could go home if she needed to.

I took her home and grabbed a beer while I was there. Annette was lying on the bed. She said, "I know you're going to hate me for this, but I really want to do it just one last time." She was referring to smoking crack. I told her that I didn't know anyone who could hook her up but she said that she knew that I could get it if I wanted to. She pleaded with me, on and on, so I finally said OK to get her off the subject, but I really had no intention of trying because of my love for her and, besides, crack and unborn babies are a very risky combination. Then we made love and I left to go back to work.

Back at work, everyone was disappointed because they figured that, due to Annette's "sickness", the party was off, so we planned to postpone it until the next day when, hopefully, she would be feeling better.

When I got home, after work, it looked like there was a party going on downstairs at Luke's. As I drove up, I could see Annette running up the stairs to our apartment. I walked inside and could see a bunch of people in Luke's place, but I passed on by and went straight upstairs. I found Annette at the kitchen table, sitting there as though she had been there a long time. I went to the fridge for a beer and she said: "You didn't get any rock, did you?" I told her no. Then I asked her what she had been doing all night while I was at work. She said that she'd been sleeping most of the time and that Luke had stopped in to tell her that there'd probably be a party downstairs, later on. I told her that I'd seen her going up the stairs when I pulled up. She said that she had gone down there for just a minute to see what they were up to and that, if I wanted to, I could go down there for a while, but that she didn't want to.

I went down to check it out, but when I got there, there was no one there. Even Luke was gone and the door was locked. Damn! It was all too clear. Could it be that Annette had been smoking crack with these people and, knowing that I don't approve, they all bailed when I got home? And, to make matters worse, I knew that Annette didn't have any money, so how did she pay for it?

I went upstairs, back to the kitchen, where I sat down at the table with Annette and continued drinking my beer. Annette was really chatty, just the way she always is when she's been smoking crack. Now it was really adding up. I didn't want to face it, so I just drank until I passed out.

The following morning I got up and was determined not to say anything to Annette about what I suspected, because I didn't want to have a big argument with her, after all, she would surely be in major denial. When it was time for my morning bath, I retrieved a fifth of vodka from its hiding place in the freezer and took it and a bottle of beer into the bathroom with me.

Sitting in the bathtub, I was trying to drown out the total reality of my situation: being on the run, Annette's crack addiction, having lost all of my friends and ties to home and not knowing if and when or how all of this might end.

After my bath, I really wasn't myself. I wanted to have a romp with Annette but she wasn't in the mood, so I went on a rampage and proceeded to destroy our bedroom. Then I passed out and threw up all over the bed and myself. When Annette came in and cleaned up the mess, I told her that I guessed that I had had a little too much to drink and that I was really sorry. She went downstairs to use Luke's phone and called Frank's to tell them that we'd be a little late for work. I felt really reassured, knowing that no matter what sort of an ass I made of myself, she'd always be there for me.

We got to work ten minutes late. I was in a world of my own. I did my work but I was numb to everyone and everything around me. It seemed as though that night would never end. Ryan said that he'd like to drop by for a while after work and I told him OK.

Later, at home, Ryan stopped by and we drank some beer and mostly talked about work. We stayed in the kitchen and Annette went on to bed in a little while. When Ryan left, I, too, went to bed. Annette was awake and was complaining about the heat. All of the windows were nailed shut, but I managed to get one of them open and I put a fan into it. When I tried to open a second one to get a cross draft, my hand slipped and broke the glass causing a deep cut in my wrist. I went to the kitchen and started applying pressure with a washcloth. Annette took one look at the cut and got sick and had to run to the bathroom. I grabbed a fresh beer and sat down at the kitchen table and wondered what my dad would do in a case like this. He was a medic in Vietnam and he probably would have stitched it up for me. Just then, Annette returned from the bathroom and wanted to know what she could do to help. I remembered the first aid kit that my dad had put into the car for me but I couldn't explain where it was stashed to Annette, so I went down and got it. I found some gauze and some tape and some disinfectant, which I used to dress the cut. After cleaning up the mess and having a few more beers, we went back to bed.

The next morning I went to see Frank and showed him the cut. I told him that I wasn't sure if I could work that day. He said that there is a doctor not too far from there and that I should go and let him have a look at it. I said, "Sure", and left, but in reality a doctor was the last thing that I had planned to spend any money on.

I went back home and started drinking. Annette wasn't scheduled to work that day. We sat on the veranda and discussed our situation, in general. I felt like the community at large was becoming way too involved in our affairs and that it wouldn't be long before someone might notice who we really were and that we were on the run. We started discussing the possibilities of relocating once again. Annette didn't want to go west, to California, because she was fearful of breaking down somewhere in the desert, so we decided to go east, toward Louisiana.

Later that evening, we had our minds pretty well made up. My wrist was killing me, so Annette did the packing. While she was packing, the landlord came by to collect the rent. Annette answered the door, but quickly referred him to me because she was too scared to talk to him; after all, we were in the process of packing to leave. I told him that I had just opened a new account and that all of my money was there and that I hadn't gotten my checks yet, but that, if he really needed the money, I would go and withdraw the cash the following day. His response was that, due to the inconvenience that this had caused him, he would have to wait an additional month before he would install a window air conditioner in the place and then he left. He also said that he charges ten dollars apiece to repair broken windows.

We packed up everything but the beer; then we made love for what would be the last time and went to sleep.

We got up extra early the next morning and loaded everything into the car. Our anticipation of starting anew was running high. We just knew that we had learned so much about life and independence that we were certain everything would work out. We figured that we could soon marry, as the age of consent in Louisiana is only seventeen. All we had to do was last just one more year and everything would be okay.

Our little cooler was too small to hold all of the beer, so we packed it in a duffel bag. We made one last check of the apartment to make sure that we had not forgotten anything. Annette wanted to throw her waitress uniform into the trash but I didn't think that would be a good idea. I felt that would be like a slap in the face, after all, these people had been very kind to us.

I felt that we should pay the rent for the week and a half that we had occupied the apartment. I counted out fifty one-dollar bills and placed them in the refrigerator, weighted down by a bottle of beer. I hoped that the landlord would understand.

On the way out of town, we saw one of the cooks from Frank's and waved good-bye to him. We knew that it wouldn't be long before everyone found out that we had left. We stopped at a gas station to fill up and got some ice for the cooler and then got onto the Interstate, headed for Louisiana.

After four or five hours of driving hand-in-hand, we needed to fill up again. We pulled off the Interstate and found a gas station. I filled the tank and, as we were walking into the store to pay for the gas, we noticed a man standing in front of a van. He had a "teardrop" tattoo under his left eye. This really upset us. We took this as a really bad omen, because, as far as I know, people with this type of tattoo have either done hard time or killed someone. But we shrugged it off and went on into the store. That's when Annette suggested that I should get a new hat because the one I was wearing had the name of the restaurant in Virginia, where I used to work, embroidered on it. She picked out a gray Calvin Klein ™ cap for me and I really liked it. We paid for it and for the gas and were back on our way.

By early afternoon we had reached the Louisiana border. I was finishing the one and only beer I had had all day. I asked Annette to get me another, but she wouldn't, she said that she didn't want me drinking too much while I was driving, that I could drink all I wanted, only later.

As we were cruising along the Interstate, doing the speed limit of seventy miles per hour, I saw a red Ford Mustang ahead, pulled over on the shoulder. As we passed it, it immediately pulled out behind us. It took a few moments to get up to highway speed, but once there, it stayed several cars behind us. I changed lanes and he followed. I was beginning to get nervous. Then I changed lanes again and, once again, he followed. Now I was really getting nervous, so I signaled to take the next exit. That's when a black Ford Bronco appeared right behind me and, suddenly, bright blue lights began flashing from behind it's grill.

Chapter Fourteen

The Long Way Back

Annette noticed that I was pulling off onto the shoulder on the off-ramp and asked me what I was doing. I told her that we were being pulled over.

As soon I stopped the car, there were officers dressed in SWAT ("Special Weapons and Tactics") gear on both sides of the car. One of the officers asked me if I knew why we had been stopped. I told him no, and he said: "For making an improper lane change." Then he asked to see my license and I told him that I had forgotten it in Virginia and that we were just on our way back home from our honeymoon, because we had just gotten married. After that, he asked me what my Social Security number is. I rattled off some fictitious numbers. Next, he asked me to step out of the car, while two officers covered the passenger side. I heard the main officer call my license plate number in to the dispatcher over his two-way radio.

Still clutching Annette's hand, they pried me out of the car. I was ushered to the rear of the car. That's when I realized that their "team" consisted of the Mustang, the Bronco and a Corvette and, right then, a marked patrol car with an officer and a dog was pulling up.

It took them a while to hear back from their dispatcher regarding the status of my license. Once the information started coming in on the Bronco's computer, they had all the goods on me. Apparently all of the Virginia Drug Task Force's bogus charges had been placed on the National Crime Information Center's (NCIC) computerized database.

At this point the lead officer confronted me about Annette. He said: "This is not your wife, this is a juvenile runaway and there is a bench warrant out for her as well as several warrants for you. I told him that there had to be some mistake, that all of my charges had been "taken care of" by the Governor's Drug Task Force in Virginia. That's when they said that that's not what the record shows and then they spun me around, slammed me onto the trunk of my car and cuffed my hands behind my back. Then I was pulled back up and marched to the marked patrol car. Annette was going off as I walked away saying that it's all over now. The officer told me to face forward and then he shoved me into the patrol car and my hat flew from my head. He picked it up and threw it into the back of the car where I was lying across the seat. That's when I told the officer that he's just taken away everything that's ever meant anything to me.

As soon as I was in the back of the patrol car, the uniformed officer got into the front and took off with me. He was going very fast and had the lights and siren blaring. The last thing I remember seeing at the scene, is Annette being escorted into the Bronco.

Before I knew it, we had arrived at the Sulphur, Louisiana City Jail. There, I was escorted through a steel door into the booking area. From there I was placed in a holding cell that had no bench or bunk. All there was, was a stainless steel toilet and a metal ring bolted to the floor. I paced back and forth in this ten by twelve foot cage for a few minutes until I heard a great deal of commotion coming from the booking area. One of the jail's trustees walked by and I asked him what was going on. He said that they were bringing in some girl and that she was making a real fuss.

In a little while one of the officers in the SWAT gear came and got me and took me back up front, to the booking area. On the way, we passed an interrogation room where I could see Annette standing at the little window in the door; she was crying and saying that she loved me. I mouthed the words, "I love you too", and kept on walking because the officer was yanking me along and telling me that there was a telephone call for me.

In a moment we arrived in a conference room where the rest of their Task Force was waiting and then someone handed me the phone. On the phone was Jerry from Virginia. He asked me if I had really thought that I could get away with this and that he had never believed me when I told them that I had sold my car because, he believed, that I probably loved that car more than I loved Annette. I couldn't have disagreed more. I asked him to clarify for me, how much trouble I was actually in, and how much trouble was Annette in. He told me that all of my Virginia charges would still be "taken care of", but that it was very important to the Task Force that I return and be available to testify against all of the people who I had participated in busting. He also said that Annette's mom really wanted her home and that she wasn't really in a whole lot of trouble, that she might have to do a month, at most, in a juvenile facility but that she really didn't have that much to worry about. Then he went on to say that I shouldn't make it hard on myself, that I should just go ahead and waive extradition; otherwise I would end up being locked up a whole lot longer than necessary.

They took me back to the holding cell. On the way, I passed Annette's room again. She was still crying. I told her not to do anything stupid and to just go ahead and waive extradition, that it would save her a whole lot of trouble in the long run. Not that I had a whole lot of time to talk, as they were pushing me along, down the hallway and then they threw me back into the cell. I could still hear Annette screaming at the top of her lungs, that we'll always be together, always.

After a while, one of the trustees brought me a bologna sandwich with mustard and a slice of tomato and a plastic cup of Kool Aid. Later on a guard came and got me and took me back to the booking area where he wanted to verify my name and birth date. When he asked me for my Social Security number, I told him that I didn't know it but that it is the same as my driver's license number. He thought that I was being smart with him so he took me back to the cell.

About an hour later, this same guard came back and took me to the booking area again. He wanted to know if I was ready to cooperate yet. I told him that I have been cooperating to the best of my ability. When he got to the question about the Social Security number again, I answered just as I had before. This time he accepted my answer. Then he asked me where I was born and I told him, Florida. He wanted to know *where* in Florida and I told him that I didn't really know, so he took me back to the cell again.

Several hours later, a trustee with a key came and got me and took me back up to booking once more. He told me that it would be best if I just cooperated with the officer. I told him that I had been trying my best to cooperate, but that the officer just didn't understand. He also mentioned that he had heard that there was a car title in my personal property envelope and he wanted to know all about the car. I told him all about my '86 Nissan 300 ZX with the chrome rims and tinted windows. He seemed to know that I wouldn't be needing the car for a while and wanted to know what I was planning to do with it. I told him that I hadn't really had a chance to give it much thought. He suggested that I should think about maybe selling it because I probably wouldn't be coming back to Louisiana for a while and anyway, I probably wouldn't be able to afford the storage fees for any length of time.

When we got to the booking area, the officer told the trustee to fingerprint me. The trustee remarked that, apparently I was used to this, since I was offering all of the correct fingers in the correct order.

Finally, the officer returned and told the trustee to leave. Then he took me into one of the interrogation rooms and said, because of my Virginia charges, that he would have to search me before I could be placed with the main population of his jail. He advised me that, in Louisiana, the penalty for bringing a controlled substance into a correctional facility is an automatic fifteen years, so if I knew what was good for me, I would turn it over now. I tried to explain to him that he had nothing to worry about, that I haven't messed with that stuff since I left Virginia.

Now it was time to be thoroughly searched. The first thing that the officer said was: "I am not a faggot, my name is officer..." Then he told me to take off my shoes and turn my socks inside out. Next, he had me remove my belt and discovered the secret compartment that contained about a hundred dollars. Then I had to empty my pockets where I had about four hundred dollars and my pager. Finally, he told me to take off my pants and shirt and to turn them inside out also. When he was satisfied that I had nothing more to hide, he placed my personal belongings in a bag marked with my name and then he let me put my clothes back on and sent me to the laundry room with the trustee where I was issued a pair of orange pants and an orange shirt. My clothes were placed in a bag with my name on it and locked away. Next, they gave me a sheet, pillowcase and a pillow and a blanket and then I was escorted back to the booking area.

In a little while the officer came and escorted me to a cell. There was one other guy in the cell. He had been sleeping until the officer opened the cell door. He awakened briefly, just long enough to introduce himself as "Dude". I introduced myself and he rolled over and went back to sleep on his lower bunk. I made up the upper bunk and took a few minutes to get my bearings.

From my vantage point I could see three other cells. The walls were made of brown stone and the floors were concrete and dirt. The steel bars extended from the floor to the graffiti filled ceiling. My cell had the customary stainless steel plumbing fixture and a steel bench was bolted to the floor and wall.

Two guys were housed in the cell directly across from mine. I asked them about making telephone calls and a trustee said that he would get me the phone. In a few minutes he came back with a pay phone mounted on a rolling cart and pushed it to where I could reach it through the bars. I picked up the phone and dialed my dad's number. He said that someone from the Virginia Governor's Drug Task Force had called him earlier that day to ask him to give me a message in case I called him. They wanted me to know that I still had some "unfinished business" there and that they really needed me to contact them. I also told my dad that I thought that Annette is pregnant. He did not welcome this news at all. We really did not talk that long because this phone had an automatic time limit and the time quickly ran out.

The rest of the night, until around three or four in the morning, was spent talking to the guys across the way and to the trustees who really had the run of the place. While I tossed and turned restlessly, my thoughts turned, once again, to Annette and all we could have had. Actually, these thoughts of Annette became my saving grace, the only thing that kept me going.

Early the next morning I awoke when a trustee announced that breakfast had arrived. Hot pancakes and syrup and some kind of juice.

After breakfast we had to sweep and mop our cells and then I went back to bed. After a while a trustee came by and unlocked our cell and announced that we were needed in the booking area. When we got there, there were several other prisoners in shackles. An officer informed us that we were going to court and then we were handcuffed and shackled also.

We were placed in a secure van and driven to the courthouse. In the van I was talking to another prisoner who had just been arrested that morning. He told me that he had just seen my picture on that morning's news and how he'd heard the story that we'd finally been apprehended. I really didn't believe him.

At the courthouse some of the other prisoners got a chance for a quick smoke during the walk from the van to court. Once inside, we were placed in a windowless room with six chairs, one for each of us. In a little while we were escorted to the courtroom where we were seated in the jury box, an empty chair between each one.

One by one, our names were called, and we would rise and stand in front of the bench. Now I finally learned what charges had been brought against me: two minor traffic violations, contributing to the delinquency of a minor and conspiracy. I asked the judge, "What about my Virginia charges?" His reply: "I don't know nuthin' about what you're talkin' about, boy." Then he asked me if I wanted a lawyer or if I wanted to waive my right to counsel. I told him that I couldn't afford a lawyer and that I would like the court to appoint a public defender. He sent me to the clerk's desk where I had to sign some papers. When all of us had been processed in this way, we got back into the van and returned to the jail. On the way back one of the prisoners told me to be careful. He said that the cops would probably want to beat the shit out of me because of Annette's age. He said: "Don't try to fight them, that would just make it worse."

It was time for lunch when we arrived back at the jail. Some kind of beef with rice and gravy; they called it "gumbo."

Before I knew it, I was called back up to the booking area where two police officers and a guard were waiting. After patting me down, the skinny one cuffed and shackled me and escorted me outside to a waiting patrol car where he patted me down again and checked the cuffs and the shackles to make sure that they were secure.

The two officers placed me in the back seat of the car and they got into the front. It was really spooky, we just drove on and on without saying a word. Finally, I broke the silence and told them that the Virginia Governor's Drug Task Force members were aware of where I was and that they were working on getting me back to Virginia as soon as possible. That's when they pulled in to an oil field and turned the car around. At this

119

point their demeanor changed and they began bragging about some of the drug busts that they had been involved in and how they recruited their informants.

Eventually we arrived at a large office building somewhere downtown. They escorted me inside. The skinny one made a wise crack about my hair. Referring to my hair coloring, he said: "I hope you only did that to disguise your appearance." The elevator took us to the third floor where they took me into a judge's office. The judge wanted to know if I was planning to waive extradition. I told him yes. He said that that was good, because he didn't want my ass in his city anyway. I signed the waiver and then the officers took me back to the jail.

Back at the jail, my cellmate had been promoted to trustee and had been moved to a different area. Now I had the whole cell to myself!

That afternoon an older trustee came around and asked if I wanted to buy anything from the jail's canteen store. I requested some fruit pies and some real sodas. I was enjoying my snack when the trustee from the first day came by. He offered to buy my car for five hundred dollars. He said that his brother had gone to look at it and that the clutch seemed to have a problem and that there was some kind of minor damage to the front end. I told him that the clutch had been having problems for a while but that it was driveable. As far as the damage, that must have happened when they towed the car in. I told him OK, that I would sign over the title when he brought me the money.

Dinner, a cold sandwich and Kool Aid, came and went. That night I got a new cellmate, Tony. He was barely eighteen. He told me that they had pulled him in for violating probation, but I'm not sure what he was on probation for. He said that his probation officer had called him to come in to his office to sign some papers and that, when he got there, he was surrounded by cops and arrested.

We talked most of the night about our ladies and even suggested that we all get together after all of this is over and maybe set up housekeeping, until the guard came by and told us to be quiet. Later on, he came by again and said that he's glad that Virginia knew where I was because, if it had been up to him, he would have strung me up in some swamp and left me there for the 'gators. The third time he came back to quiet us down, he opened the cell door and motioned for me to come with him. I asked if I needed my shirt or my shoes and he just shook his head, no. He escorted me back the barren cell where I was first held on the first day. There he told me to get down on my knees and then he cuffed one of my hands and then passed the handcuffs through the metal ring that was bolted to the floor and then he cuffed the other hand. He did the same with shackles around my ankles. This is how I spent the rest of the night.

This night was pure hell. I was chained to this bull-ring on the floor and I couldn't even lie down, I just squatted there, on the cold concrete floor, all night long. Once again, memories of prior abandonment abounded. I tried hard to find comfort in thoughts of Annette, but this time I was hurting just too damn much.

I was glad when I was released back to my cell although it was a while before I was able to straighten my knees and my back without pain. Little did I know that I would be spending several more nights chained to that bull-ring, in fact, it would be this guy's routine for me every time he was on duty.

A few days later the trustee who wanted to buy my car came up with the money and I signed over the title to him. His brother had come by for this occasion. He said that there were still sixty or seventy beers in the car. I was able to arrange to have most of my clothes and other belongings packed up and brought to the jail, but they wouldn't allow my set of chef's knives to be brought in. The trustee's brother offered to keep them for me until my dad could have them shipped home.

Later on I telephoned Annette's mom. She said that she knew for a fact that Annette isn't pregnant. I told her how much I still loved Annette and how much she will always mean to me. She said: "You can't always have what you want." I asked her where they were keeping Annette and she said that she's in some juvenile facility. Lastly, she told me that Barney was planning to come to Louisiana to bring both Annette and me back to Virginia.

Finally, on the tenth day, I was told that my transportation back to Virginia had been arranged. I was anxious to collect all of my belongings and clothes for the long trip back and was very hopeful that I might see Annette again soon. Two Virginia State Troopers, in plain clothes, had arrived to bring me back. They had all of my stuff in an interrogation room. They took me in there and one of them asked me if I had a jacket. I said yes. That's when he told me to get it and that that was all that I was allowed to take along. Then I asked him if I could just bring along an audio-tape and he replied: "I guess we're already having a communication problem", and then he walked out and locked the door. He came back with his partner in a few minutes. They patted me down and handcuffed me and took me outside and placed me in the back of their rental car.

Once in the car, one of the officers showed me the order for my return. He said that this could be done the easy way, or the hard way. He said that all that was required was that my carcass be returned to Middlesex County, Virginia, dead or alive. We drove to a small airport, seemingly in the middle of nowhere. When I stepped out of the car, one of the officers explained what the jacket was really meant for, to hide the handcuffs.

Once inside the terminal lobby, the officers went to the ticket counter, showed their credentials and explained that I was a fugitive from Virginia and that they had me in custody and were taking me back. The ticket agent asked if they also had the female subject with them. They said no, that they didn't know anything about that and they hustled me away, over to the other side of the building.

As I sat waiting, I could see Annette, accompanied by a male and a female escort, as she rounded the corner of the lobby. She had no luggage and wasn't handcuffed. I tried not to look in her direction because I was having a really hard time holding back the tears. Just then, one of the troopers asked me if that was her, and I just nodded with a big lump in my throat.

When it came time to board the plane, the security staff cleared the area of all other passengers and I was escorted onto the plane first. We went all the way to the rear of the plane where they placed me next to a window and then they, too, were seated. Now the rest of the passengers were allowed to board.

When Annette was brought on board it was evident that no arrangements for an escort for her had been made. This was really a problem for the pilot. He told the female chaperone that it is against company policy for subjects in custody to be on their plane without supervision. The lady asked the troopers if they would mind watching Annette until the plane landed in Dallas. They agreed and so Annette got into the window seat right across from me with the two troopers between us.

On the plane, Annette and I were not allowed to speak with each other so Annette would speak very loudly to the officer by her side, intending for me to hear. Basically, she was telling him that she felt assured that she was not looking at a whole lot of trouble once she got back, that she might possibly have to spend, maybe a month or so, in a juvenile facility.

After a while, we were able to communicate by simply "mouthing" words without actually making a sound. We were reassuring each other that we still loved each other more than anything and that our plans to be together could still be fulfilled, once all of this mess is over with. She even told me that her mother would now give permission for her to marry me. I asked her if she had been able to confirm her pregnancy and she said yes. Finally, one of the troopers got tired of this and said that their watching Annette was strictly a favor and that, if we didn't knock it off, they would have the plane turn around and take her back to Sulphur.

In Dallas, a woman got on the plane and took custody of Annette, taking her off the plane first. After the rest of the passengers got off, it was my turn, one trooper in front of me and one behind.

We took an airport shuttle to another part of the airport. Annette and her chaperone were seated in the back. Unfortunately, it was standing-room-only for me. The ride was very bumpy and erratic and I couldn't hold on to anything because of how I was handcuffed, so the troopers, sort of, had to hold me up. Each time, when I would nearly fall, one of them would grab onto me.

Finally we arrived at our stop. I took one last glance at Annette before they rushed me inside and away. Next, we boarded another shuttle; this one was a light rail consisting of several cars. This car was packed full too. I was standing next to some "preppie" office worker. Every time the car would jerk around, I would fall into him. Finally he became very annoyed and asked me why I didn't just hold on to the handrail above. I slid the jacket, which had been concealing the handcuffs, high up on my arms. The guy took one look and got this terrified expression on his face, then he literally fought his way to the other end of the car as fast as he could.

We arrived at our boarding area, but it was not yet time to board. While we were waiting we made small talk. One of the troopers wanted to know what had happened to my wrist (the one I had cut on the bedroom window). I told him about being chained to the floor in the Sulphur City Jail and let him assume that that's where it happened. At this point he took pity on me and removed the cuffs with a stern warning, not to do anything stupid.

Our plane was finally ready to board and we went through the same routine as before, the troopers and I boarded while the rest of the passengers were kept away. Of course, we had to sit all the way in the back again. I saw no sign of Annette.

During the flight, my mind was on what Annette and I had been through and what might lie ahead. Surely, by now, everyone knew exactly what I had done to get my charges dropped. And what did Barney mean by "unfinished business?"

Chapter Fifteen

The Pink Room

When we arrived in Norfolk, Virginia all of the other three hundred passengers were let off the plane first. Then I was told to put on my jacket and I was handcuffed with the link-chain of the cuffs passed through and underneath my belt to further limit the use of my hands and arms. The flight attendant remarked to one of the troopers, "Well, I guess your day is about over now." The trooper responded that it really wasn't because there could always be surprises. The stewardess gave me a look, as if to say: "Is this guy really on the level?"

On our way through the airport lobby, a little kid maybe five or six years old, hit me on the leg with his fist. His mother, noticing that I was in handcuffs and under heavy escort, quickly yanked him away. Outside, one trooper stood and held me by my arm while the other went to get a rental car.

On the way back to Saluda, I told my keepers that I hadn't eaten anything since last night except for the peanuts on the plane. They weren't really sympathetic, saying that they weren't planning to stop anywhere else until they were rid of me.

Barney was waiting for us in front of the Sheriff's office in Saluda when we arrived. I could hardly wait to get out of the car and the handcuffs; after all, Jerry had told me that I wouldn't be facing any additional charges when I got back.

They took me inside and handed the brown paper envelope, which contained my personal property, to Barney. They spent only a couple of minutes telling Barney about the trip and then they were gone. I was sure glad to see them go; now it was time for me to be gone, too.

I was sitting in the "guest" chair in front of the magistrate's desk and Barney was standing behind me when a deputy walked in and sat down at the desk. He had several papers, which he placed on the desk in front of him, and then he began to read them to me. That's when I learned that I was being charged with two misdemeanor counts of "contributing to the delinquency of a minor" that were initiated by Annette's mother and one count of "failure to appear" for not appearing in court for the bogus conspiracy charge stemming from the controlled sale of the seven pounds of marijuana to Lana. Hell, they had even told me at the time, that the "charge" was only brought to make it look convincing, and that I didn't really have to appear because it would not be prosecuted.

When the deputy had finished reading the charges and advising me that I was under arrest, the magistrate arrived. He told me that he could not set any bail on the "failure to appear" charge and that I would have to go to jail until court convened in a few days and then the case would be decided by a judge.

I turned to Barney and asked him how in the hell they expected me to be locked up with all of the people I had set up, and countless more who weren't sure but were mad enough that they didn't give a shit, they just wanted someone to fuck up. The magistrate broke in and said that he understood how I felt threatened, but not to worry. He said that there was a specially segregated facility on the other side of West Point (VA) where inmates at "high risk", such as "informants and child molesters" were housed. That's just great if you've been convicted of something and sentenced to prison, but what happens to me *now*? Barney, with his usual "oh well" attitude, quickly changed the subject and asked me if I wanted him to run to a nearby fast-food place and pick me up something to eat. I told him no, that food was the farthest thing from my mind right then. Then he pulled a bunch more papers out of a folder and told me that he had warrants for me charging me with "conspiracy" stemming from every single time that I had talked with Jerry and others about buying or selling marijuana prior to the time when they actually brought me "into the fold." He even had a conspiracy warrant for me stemming from my involvement in Lana's set-up.

How could Barney think that I'd be interested in a burger at a time like this? Burger? Hell, right then I'd have given anything just to be able to die instantly, rather than have to face the inevitable.

Well, they fingerprinted me umpteen times and then they carted me off to the jail where they removed my shoes and placed me in a small holding cell. As he was leaving, Barney told the jail officer that I was not to be allowed to have contact with any other inmates until further notice.

A female guard brought me into an interview room for the usual intake questions. She already seemed to have quite a bit of background on me, as she was familiar with my street name, "Paco". She asked if I had any serious enemies and I said "probably so" and told her that many of them were probably right here, in the same jail. At the conclusion of the interview, she let me use a telephone to call my dad. I asked him to be sure to let Annette know that I still loved her very much, but that I didn't think that I'd ever get to see her again. I had to end the call quickly for fear of breaking down right then and there, and that's one thing that you *don't* want to do in jail.

Next came the obligatory shower and then I was issued my orange wardrobe with matching rubber flip-flops. They handed me a Jail Rulebook, a plastic mattress, blanket, pillow and linens and soap, toothbrush and toothpaste, all of which, except for the mattress was contained in a plastic milk crate. After two or three more hours in the little holding cell, a guard came and got me and my stuff.

I ended up in an "isolation" cell but one other inmate already occupied it. This really puzzled me because I distinctly remembered Barney instructing the staff that I was not to have contact with any other inmates.

I was not new to this cell, as I had spent a day or two here on my previous visit to this facility; it was the pink room, again. The lower bunk was available, so that's where I put my mattress. I was too beat to make the bed up with the linens; in fact I didn't really give a shit if I just curled up and died, so I threw the blanket over it and lay down.

My cellmate looked and acted like some kind of forgotten person, almost wild, like a prisoner of war. He stood around 5'5", was slightly muscular and his skin tone obviously hadn't seen much daylight for some time. I guess that the guy must have been suffering from some sort of mental imbalance as he would jump up onto the bars and make strange animal noises and grunt, everyone called him "Swifty". The nurse brought him medication three times a day. I asked him several times, what the meds were for, and each time he had a different explanation.

As soon as I had lain down on my bunk, Swifty began to ask me all about my situation. He said that he remembered me from the last time that I was here, that he had been in the cell beside this one, and that he had only had contact with me through the wall and had wondered what I looked like. He remembered that they had brought me in for possessing a quarter pound of marijuana the first time, and that he just knew that I'd be back. Just then, a guard came and ordered me out of the cell and told me to bring everything along. He took me back up front to the little holding cell. Apparently, during shift change, somebody discovered that I was supposed be in isolation, not in a cell with any other inmate.

I spent the rest of that night scrunched up in that little cell. The mattress was even too long to fit on the floor. Trying hard to get to sleep, I couldn't help wondering what sort of sleeping arrangements Annette had tonight. For nearly two months, I had shared my bed with her, showered with her and shared her every thought.

I awoke around six or so when the trustees who were on "work release" were being let out of the door. I was folded up like a jack knife and pretty much unable to move. They offered me breakfast but I wasn't interested; for without Annette, I only wanted to die.

After a while, one of the jail administrators came by. She explained that a mistake had been made on the previous night, when I was placed in the cell with Swifty, but that, for now, they really didn't have any other choice because no other isolation cells were available and anyway, Swifty was not one of the people who I needed to worry about, that he was basically harmless.

So they took me back to the pink room. Swifty really wasn't a problem, as he was asleep most of the time. I think that the medication may have had something to do with that.

Three days later I was taken to court. This was the day of my arraignment on all of the charges except those involving Annette; those would be heard later, in the Juvenile Court. This day the judge read all of the charges against me, advised me that if I was found guilty, that I could go to prison and that I had the right to be represented by an attorney and so on. I requested a court-appointed lawyer and Mr. Rose was appointed.

Mr. Rose took me into the jury room to find out more about my case. Apparently he had spoken with the prosecutor before my case was called, because he seemed to have a great deal of information already. He said that the Commonwealth was willing to waive all of the charges that he had been appointed to represent me on, as long as I promised to be the Commonwealth's witness in all of the cases in which I had been involved with the task force. Furthermore, he said that if I didn't cooperate with the Commonwealth in this way, all of the current charges, the ones that he represented me on, would be prosecuted to the fullest. Feeling that I had absolutely no choice in the matter, I promised to cooperate.

Nearly a month went by. My trial date in the Circuit Court came and went. On the day of the trial I wondered why no one had come to get me. I kept trying to tell the guards that I was supposed to have my trial, but they just said that they knew nothing about it. I wondered if I had been forgotten. Not even Barney, my greatest "advocate", had been around to see me.

I had heard something about "electronic in-home incarceration". That's when they fasten a radio transmitter to your ankle and call you on the telephone at random times to make sure that you're at home. It sounded good to me, so I called my dad to discuss the possibility. His response was, "To be on house arrest, first you've got to have a house." To me, this was just another reason why I just wanted to be dead. I didn't realize, at the time, that I was actually much safer in jail than I would have been at home, especially with my dad gone all day.

While I had use of the phone, I decided to give Annette's mom a call. I was really curious to know how she was doing and when she would be free, after all, she's been in a juvenile detention facility near Williamsburg ever since they brought us back. Her mom told me that Annette had had a miscarriage shortly after entering the Louisiana detention facility and that she didn't want me to have any contact with her, at least for as long as she had anything to say about it and to never call her house again. I pleaded with her, telling her that this would not only hurt me very deeply, but also Annette, since we both needed each other desperately. I even tried to bargain with her, to give it a rest until all this mess was behind us, but she would have none of it. I asked her, what about a few years from now, after Annette turns eighteen? She said that that was a long time off and that Annette would surely be over me by then. How did she presume to know that Annette would be over me by then? It was as if she was planning to change Annette's mind herself, one way or another.

The day of the Juvenile Court trial finally came. The courtroom is on the second floor of the Civil War era courthouse. I was parked in the holding cell behind the courtroom, just off the back stairway adjacent to the tiny elevator. There is a small grid in the holding cell door. I heard the elevator doors open and went to take a look. There I saw Annette, accompanied by a female attendant from the detention center. She stopped in front of the door momentarily and our eyes met. I heard her tell the lady, "That's my boyfriend in there." Since there is only one holding cell, the lady had to stand with Annette in the hallway right outside the door. The whole time, while we were waiting to go into the courtroom, our eyes remained fixated on one another. Eventually a deputy came and moved Annette to the jury room. That's when the prosecutor came to talk to me. He said that Annette really didn't want to have to testify against me and that he would be willing to drop one of the two charges if I would agree to plead guilty to the other one. I said that I'd have to think about it and that, since I didn't have a lawyer, I'd let him know my answer when the case was called.

When the case was finally called, the judge read the charges against me once again and asked me how I wished to plead. "Guilty, your honor." At that point, the prosecutor rose from his chair and told the judge that, by pre-trial agreement in return for a guilty plea to one of the charges, he was dismissing the other one.

Back in the pink room, I finally began to realize that I really would never get to see Annette again, especially since her mother seemed to be doing everything in her power to keep us apart and to turn her against me. Anyway, Annette was getting ready to be released from detention and I had no idea, whatsoever, how long I would be locked up. It seemed like the powers-that-be were making up the rules as they went along, and I really didn't know whom I could count on or trust anymore.

It was time for lunch and I told the guard that I didn't want it; that I wasn't eating. Less than an hour had passed when the guard returned. He told that there was someone he wanted me to talk to, and he took me to the library. That's where a mental health clinician was waiting. She asked me what was troubling me and said that she was concerned about my refusal to eat. I told her that I just didn't want to eat. She said: "You've got to eat to live", to which I responded: "Well, maybe I don't feel like living." She said that nothing could be *that* bad. We ended up talking for about an hour and I told her about how much losing Annette was hurting me and that my own dad didn't even want me in the house. She said that she had trouble accepting that and that he was probably just angry about the embarrassment that this whole thing has undoubtedly caused him. I told her my take on that. I told her that, I believed it's sort of like a dog that shits on a rug; after a while, the owner gets tired of cleaning up after him and throws him out. Then she asked me how many times I had shit on his rug. I said: "Quite a few." Apparently she had heard of some of my exploits from other inmates. She asked me, "What do you expect; where else do you think you belong?" To which I replied, "I guess I don't *belong* anywhere. She concluded by saying that I'll get through this, one way or another, and when I do get out, if Annette's there for me, OK, but if she's not, I'll just have to go on. When dinner arrived that evening, I did not refuse.

A few days passed and I had been eating OK. The day came for the trial for possessing the quarter pound of marijuana that I was busted for in Chapter One. It was July 30, 1998. As I waited in the holding cell, the lawyer who had been appointed by the court to represent me in this case, Mr. Gatsby came in to talk with me. He told me that he had been negotiating a plea agreement with the prosecutor. In the agreement, I would plead guilty to felony possession of marijuana with the intent to distribute same. In return for my guilty plea, the court would sentence me to prison for a period of ten years with all of the time suspended for a period of five years, upon certain conditions. Those conditions included that I shall testify for the Commonwealth of Virginia in the prosecution of other drug-related cases in any jurisdiction of which I have knowledge; that I shall keep the peace, be of good behavior and not violate any laws; that I shall be on indefinite supervised probation until released by the Department of Probation and Parole, upon such terms and conditions as they may promulgate, including but not limited to, random drug screens; that I pay all court costs and other fees in this matter upon such terms as determined by the Department of Probation and Parole; that, upon my cooperation with drug investigators and the Commonwealth as aforesaid, the Commonwealth will move the court to dismiss the four other felony charges against me in Middlesex County plus two additional ones in the City of Newport News.

It all sounded good to me. Ten years, with all time suspended for cooperating with the authorities and keeping out of trouble. Sure, I'd have a felony conviction on my record, but what other choice did I really have? Even my lawyer said that it was the best I could have hoped for. Anyway, I could already feel the freedom; I just wanted out!

Confident that this horrible ordeal was just about over, I signed the plea agreement, the judge accepted it and I shook Mr. Gatsby's hand.

Back to the holding cell I went. There, Gatsby was talking to me through the mesh window. I wanted to know if this meant that it was all over now. He said that the only other reason that he knew, why I could be held in jail any longer, was to await the sentencing hearing on the juvenile case that I had pleaded guilty to earlier. This was worrisome news.

When I got back into the pink room, Swifty was taunting me, saying that I would never get out of jail; that they were just jerking me around. This really pissed me off and I couldn't stand it any longer so I went at him. We punched and kicked and slammed each other around for a while until we were both spent. No one ever came or cared what we were doing. When it was all over, we were both covered with bruises.

The Juvenile Court sentencing was scheduled for the following day. I had high hopes of freedom coming my way some time that day. The judge sentenced me to a year in jail and suspended all but the time that I had already served. She also admonished me to have no contact with Annette for a period of two years or the suspended portion of the sentence would be reinstated. With that, I was transported back to the jail.

Back at the jail I was strip-searched before being taken back to my cell. That's when the guard noticed the bruises all over my body. I told him that I had no idea how they had gotten there. He took me back to the pink room where another guard came to see Swifty and me. He said that, if we didn't tell him what had happened, how we had gotten our bruises, that he would bring in-house charges against both of us for assault on an inmate. We joked about it and played it off, saying that we had just been playing around and neither one wanted to be the one who wanted to quit first.

Later that evening, a guard came to the pink room and told me to pack it up. Could it be? Was I finally getting out of here? No, not so. I was taken to a cellblock occupied by eight or ten trustees, none of whom had been involved in any of my prior exploits working with the task force. All of the bunks were taken, so they brought in a blue neoprene pallet, which, because of their unique shape, are called "boats" by the inmates. I placed my mattress on top of the boat, placed my milk crate beside it for a "night stand" and settled in.

Chapter Sixteen

Will This Ever End?

Jail sucks. Just when I thought that I might be getting out, all they do is transfer me to a different section.

On the day before Sammy's preliminary hearing was set, Barney, Jerry and a couple of others had me called out of the block and taken to the jail superintendent's office. I was never really sure what the purpose of this visit was. First they taunted me and asked me if I was having fun yet, being locked up. I really didn't see the humor. They had confiscated my pager when I was brought back to Virginia but they had been monitoring it ever since. Now there was a strange number displayed on it, and they wanted me to call that number. The number was from Louisiana and they must have thought that it was some sort of drug-related connection. So I called the number. The person who answered was the brother of the trustee from the Sulphur City Jail who had bought my car. He was calling to find out what he should do with the briefcase containing my culinary knives. I told him that I would get a hold of my dad and ask him to give him a call to have them shipped to him.

For some time now, Barney had been talking about what a good idea it might be, for me to join the military after all of this is over. I told him that, of the four branches, I think that I would like it best in the Air Force. He said that he'd look into it for me. For some reason, he had never gotten around to it. Anyway, I figured that they wouldn't take me with a felony record. Barney kept encouraging me though. Today I wanted to know for sure what my chances might be, so he picked up the phone and supposedly called a recruiter. The "recruiter" supposedly said that, even if my felony record were expunged, I would still not qualify, simply because I had been *charged* with a felony offense. Lastly, they casually mentioned that Annette's mother had called to say that she had heard that there is now a thirty-five thousand-dollar contract out for me. Barney joked: "If Sammy didn't have enough money to make bail or to afford a lawyer, where would he come up with this kind of loot?" Actually, it makes perfect sense. You see, no dealer would ever admit to the authorities that he has bail or lawyer money, because they would confiscate all of it, calling it monies derived from the sale of drugs, unless the guy had a legit job on the side where actual earnings were possible. When all was said and done, they "treated" me to a sandwich and a shake from Hardee's™ and then sent me back to the block.

Right after breakfast the next morning, there were only two other guys and I in the block. The other trustees had left for their jailhouse jobs. One of these guys, Max, said that he had heard that I had informed on a bunch of people and he wanted to know if it was true. I told him yea I did, but that I'd only done it to people who had screwed me over in the past. He wanted to know if I knew Sammy's brother, Clarence, and I told him, yea. That's when he told me that Clarence had told him that I had informed on him (Max). I said' "Obviously, that's a bunch of shit, 'cause I don't even know you,"

My logic must have made sense to him. Then I told him about Lamont, who had been informing for some time and how he tried to make it look like it was me instead of him turning people in and how he was always saying how much he hated narks and so on. Then I asked what he had done to get busted. He said that he is an interstate trucker and that he would frequently bring back five pounds of marijuana. He said that he had gotten pulled over one night on Route 17, just outside of Saluda. There were at least four cars involved and also a drug-sniffing dog. The agents, without hesitation, went right to the exact spot where the bud was always stashed. So I asked him to think back about who else knew about this secret spot. He thought for a moment and said: "Only my wife and step-daughter." Then I asked him, "Which one is on rock?" "My step-daughter", he replied. He said that she was always hanging around Clarence, because Clarence knew where to get it (i.e. Sammy). So, anyway, it was now clear who had ratted him out and he was satisfied.

It wasn't long before they came to take me to the hearing. I was ushered into the jail's conference room where there was a white vest lying on the table. The guards told me to put it on, under my orange shirt. They said that it was Kevlar™ and that I knew why I had to wear it. They also let me wear my Nikes™, which was quite unusual, as usually all I got to wear was the orange rubber flip-flops. They walked me to the intake area and shackled my ankles, cuffed my hands and secured them to a waist chain. From here they took me to the Superintendent's office, located about a block away from the jail, and across the street from the courthouse. That's where I basically spent the rest of the day, in a chair, hands and feet shackled. Lunch came and went; dinner came and went. The only thing to do to pass the time was to shoot the breeze with my guards; one male and two females. The male guard had known my dad for quite a few years, having worked for him in a program for delinquent boys before hiring on at the jail. He was curious to know what my plans were for the future. The female guards were also wondering. I told them all about the plans that Annette and I had for the future. I told them that we had discussed my working as a cook on an off-shore oilrig or maybe a cruise ship or a freighter for a couple of years, until she turned eighteen, That way I could earn enough money for us to start our new life together. Anyway, it would not be very healthy for me to hang around here much longer. Finally, around nine o'clock they took me across the street to the heavily guarded courthouse. There were two guards in front of me and two guards behind me, escorting me up the twenty-three stairs to the courtroom.

After waiting for a few more minutes in the holding cell, they took me into the courtroom, still fully shackled, and I was placed in the witness stand. When I looked around, I saw that the courtroom had been cleared. The only ones there, besides the police, were Sammy and his lawyer, the judge, clerk and prosecutor and a couple of the guys from the task force.

I couldn't even raise my right hand to be sworn, but that didn't seem to matter as no one even attempted to swear me in. After the prosecutor had finished with me, it was the defense's turn. Sammy's lawyer, Ms. Anderson, represented to the court, that she felt that it was inappropriate for the government to pay informants to buy and sell drugs under cover and then spend the tax payers' money to try them and keep them locked up. Then she asked me why I had turned Sammy in. She wanted to know if, in my opinion, crack was worse than marijuana in some way, or what. I said that I did it because I felt like it and that, I believe, a drug is a drug, no better, no worse. And that's all there was to it. I couldn't believe it, sitting around in shackles all day, just for this moment.

That night, as I was being let back in to the block, the guys sarcastically, asked if I had brought back any bud or rock for them. You see, they actually thought that I was out with the force, busting people.

Later on that night, a new inmate arrived in our block. He had just been busted in another county for cultivating fifty marijuana plants. The next day I learned that he had been promised to be released on his own recognizance on the following day. It wasn't long before we all figured out that he had had plenty to tell Barney and the task force.

Finally, the day came for my remaining charges to be officially dismissed. I waited all day to be called to court but was continually disappointed. Breakfast, lunch and dinner all passed. Would they postpone it again? How could they? Don't they know how sick and tired I am of this GD place?

Around six o'clock I was taken from my cell to the conference room where the "bulletproof" vest laid waiting. I noticed a small tag in the collar and asked one of the guards to read it to me: "Puncture Repellent". This was the last straw. All this time I thought that somebody around here really gave a shit, but now I find that they weren't even using a real bulletproof vest. I'd probably be better off out of jail, on my own. At least I could run and hide. I told them to take their vest and shove it, so they shackled me and took me to off to court.

I sat at the defense table next to my lawyer, Mr. Rose. He rose from his chair and, together with the prosecutor, approached the judge's bench. They were all in agreement about dismissing the rest of my charges. When Mr. Rose returned to the table, I asked him, "Does this mean that I'm free to go?" He said, yes, but that I had to go back to the jail for "out-processing". On my way out of the back door of the courtroom, Barney stopped me and said to give him a call when I was ready to go home, that he would give me a ride.

Back at the jail they unshackled me and placed me in the little holding cell. Then a guard came to take me back to the block. I told him no, that I was supposed to be released. He said that that's not what *his* paperwork said. I told him that's what the *Judge* said, and then I asked to use the phone. I called Barney at his home, but he was no help, claiming that he didn't have any knowledge about what was happening and that he'll look into it in the morning. I said, "Fuck that", and hung up the phone. Next, I called my dad and explained the whole thing to him. He seemed really sympathetic this time and said that he would call the prosecutor and then he would call me back. Suddenly it seemed like every phone in the control room was ringing. I know that some of the calls were from my dad and some were from the prosecutor and maybe even the judge, I'm really not sure. All I know is that, at some point, my dad called me back and assured that everything had been taken care of. Sure enough, a few minutes later a guard verified the good news; I was going home at last! My dad had asked me if I wanted him to come and pick me up, but I told him no, that Barney had offered to do it and that I was going to hold him to it.

On the way home, Barney was telling me that being an informant could be a pretty good way of life for me, that I had a real knack for it and that the money is pretty decent. I didn't really respond to that, all the while thinking how I've finally got a chance to leave it all behind and actually have a normal life, with a normal job and a

normal outlook on life, and since I had this chance, I would try to make the best of it.

Chapter Seventeen

Unfinished Business

It was weird, finally walking up our driveway, but there were no yellow ribbons. My dad was waiting at the door and he was actually glad to have me home, hoping that I'd learned my lesson at last.

My first priority, of course, was to find out what was up with Annette. This would not be so easy, as I was under court order not to have any contact with her, or risk going back to jail. I also knew that my dad would never ignore it if he knew I was trying to call her on the phone.

I waited until my dad was at work and then I dialed Annette's number. She was at home by herself because, at the time, she was going to night school. Hearing her voice again after all this time, I was nearly overcome with emotion. We brought each other up to date about our respective sentences and sanctions. We both renewed our deep devotion to each other and vowed that we would remain true until my probation was over when we could finally be together without fear.

At first, I didn't even want to leave the house. After a couple of weeks my dad told me that, if I wanted to stay here, I'd have to help out with expenses and, anyway, I had nearly fifteen hundred dollars in fines and court costs to pay, so I had to find a job.

My driver's license was "restricted", which meant that I was only allowed to drive to and from work, to and from the probation office and to and from medical appointments. This is really weird, because how do they expect you to find a job, if your license won't let you drive to look for one?

One day my dad had off during the week and he decided to drive me around to check out some help-wanted ads for cooks that he had found in the paper. We dropped off a few resumes' and filled out applications. The next day they all called me back! Because I was still apprehensive about the price on my head, I decided to agree to an interview at the restaurant that was located farthest away from where we live. Getting hired was no problem; all I had to do was show up. My dad had an old pick-up truck that he used only occasionally, so he let me have it to drive to work. The first thing he did was to make me buy insurance in my own name.

I continued to call Annette secretly for the next few months. At first, we were telling each other how glad we were to have this chance to catch up. Then it became ever more clear to me that her promises of waiting for me and her professed love for me weren't all I had thought them to be. It had "slipped" out that she had been seeing other people and had been intimate with several. I couldn't believe my ears! She tried to rationalize her behavior by explaining that it was sort of like when two people are married and then separate, they both feel like they are free to do whatever, so long as they are not together. I tried to explain the difference to her, that *our* separation was forced on us, and that I didn't want anyone else, ever, and that I had thought that that was also the way she felt about it. Hell, even that last time when I saw her in court, she was still singing "Stand By Your Man". Now it was excruciatingly clear that she had found someone else. And to add insult to injury, now she wanted me to lie in court when it came time for Sammy's trial so that he would get off. She said that, if I didn't do this, she would never speak to me again! I told her that I was really very sorry that she felt this way and then I hung up the phone.

When this call was finally over, I sat back and realized that I've never suffered a loss before, in my entire life, that hurt as much as losing Annette. I've survived the loss of my biological family, mother, father, siblings, aunts, uncles and grandparents. I've been uprooted and relocated numerous times from home to numerous foster homes to, finally, a permanent adoptive home and lost many good friends in the process, not to mention having turned in all of my latest "friends" to the cops. This is the only person who I've ever really let into my heart and soul.

As time went on, I settled back into a routine consisting of going to work and going to appointments with my probation officer. I literally went nowhere else. Feeling sorry for myself was getting me nowhere. Finally, I was granted full driving privileges and was able to resume more social interactions. Although I've finally accepted the fact that the relationship will never again be what it once was, Annette will always be a very special and unique part of my life, a part that I would never willingly have given up.

Eventually it was time for Mac's trial. When it came my turn to testify, the testimony was very brief. Basically, I was asked to state how I had come to know Mac and what I had observed on the night when Jerry bought an ounce of Marijuana from him. I told the jury that I had known Mac since high school and that we used to be friends at one time and that, on the night in question, I did not see the transaction since I was in the bathroom at the time that it allegedly took place. Mac was found guilty of a lesser offense but the finding caused previously suspended time to be reinstated. I'm not really sure how much time he ended up serving.

When it was time for Clint's trial, Barney stopped by and picked me up and took me to the courthouse in Newport News. On the way, I asked Barney if Clint ever agreed to turn over any others. He said that, at first, he was willing to; he had even given them *my* name, but, because it had taken them so long to get back to him, he had gotten "cold" and refused.

When we arrived at the courthouse, Barney retrieved the pound of marijuana, which I had bought for Jerry from Clint, from the trunk. As we were walking toward the courthouse, we ran into Jerry. He said that we were in front of the wrong courthouse, that the one we wanted was two blocks over. So we headed towards that one and, as we were approaching, I saw Clint's car. His girlfriend was driving and she stopped in front of the courthouse and he got out of the car. As he neared the sidewalk, we both stopped in our tracks and stared at each other for a moment. Obviously, it had just dawned on him that it was I who had turned him in! He said, "Fuck", and walked on into the courthouse. Once inside the courthouse, we met with the prosecutor and went over the case. Then we entered the courtroom and sat down in the front row. There was a case being heard where another guy was facing the identical charge that Clint would be tried for shortly. He was found guilty and was sentenced to serve ten years in prison, but with five years suspended.

When it came time for Clint's hearing, the defense attorney asked the prosecutor if all of the witnesses were present. He told him yes. That's when he pled his client guilty as charged. Clint's girlfriend could be heard sobbing across the room. The sentence was the same as the other guy got, ten years with five suspended.

On the trip home I told Barney what Annette had said about changing my testimony in Sammy's case or she would never speak to me again. We decided that her source of rock must be more important to her than her love for me.

The day arrived for Sammy's trial. Barney picked me up and took me to the courthouse in Saluda. I had to wait in the holding cell until it was my turn to testify. In the end, my testimony was not even needed as the prosecutor and the defense agreed upon a plea bargain and Sammy pleaded guilty to whatever and I'm really not sure about the specifics of his sentence. I was just glad that it was over.

Lana's trial was next. She pleaded "not guilty". I really felt for her because that particular sale was intended for Mac, not Lana. Funny how things can get so screwed up. Anyway, they kept me in a chair in the back hallway during the entire trial so that I didn't really hear any of it. I was never even called to testify. The trial was filled with emotion and the jury was said to be sympathetic but, in the end, the evidence was sufficient for a conviction.

Jimmie's trial would be the last one. A meeting was held at the prosecutor's office to review the information. The prosecutor wanted to make sure that my memory of the facts was still accurate. By now, I had started working on writing this book, and the defense attorney had subpoenaed the outline and the overview. Barney pointed out that, according to the overview, my recollection was flawed, and that they, especially he, had never made me any promises in return for my cooperation and that I was damn lucky to have him, because a lot of other officers would have just let me stay in jail and rot.

When the trial finally came up, I was, of course, subpoenaed as a witness for the prosecution and, to my and to my dad's surprise, *he* (my dad) was subpoenaed as a witness for the defense.

We went into the courtroom and took seats up front. Soon Annette, her mother and her new "dork" boyfriend sat down right behind us. I could hear a little whimper from her. It was really quite awkward. Even my probation officer had been subpoenaed as a witness. Then the defense moved the court to separate all witnesses and the motion was granted. Now all of the witnesses were ushered out of the courtroom, to be called as their testimony was required.

I was seated in the back hallway behind the courtroom with the task force members and Lana and some other witnesses. My dad was outside, on the courthouse lawn, with my probation officer, Annette and her mom and boyfriend and several other witnesses.

Lana said that, at first, after she had gotten busted, she really hated me a lot, but that she has now come to realize that it was inevitable that we would all get busted sooner or later because we all were disregarding all common sense and regard for the law. She went on to say that she has completely changed her life, that even before she went to trial, she had given up all use of drugs and alcohol and that she had cut all ties with her antisocial friends.

Time passed, witnesses were called, but not Lana. Finally it was my turn. The prosecutor asked me to recall the events on the night in question. Annette had previously testified that I had wanted to have Jimmie's car and that there had been a deal whereby the task force would confiscate it during a bust and then arrange a way to transfer it to me. In reality, it was Jerry who had said how much he liked the car and how he'd like to have it for undercover use. When they finally did try to confiscate it, they found out that there was so much money owed on it that it wouldn't be worth their while, since they would have had to pay off the bank's lien.

Jimmie's court appointed public defender was campaigning for the prosecutor's job in the upcoming November, 1999 election. It was extremely important for him to make a good showing in any cases where he was opposing this prosecutor. He asked me if I had ever been under the influence of alcohol or if I had ever participated in smoking any marijuana while in the presence of any of the task force members. I said yes, that I did so in order to maintain my cover. Apparently this response was not consistent with Barney and Jerry's previous testimony. The prosecutor suddenly rose from his seat and suggested to the court that this might be a good time to recess for lunch.

I went outside and caught up with my dad. Seated on a concrete bench beside a Civil War monument, were Annette, her boyfriend and her mom. As we passed in front of them, Annette's eyes met mine. As soon as her boyfriend was aware what was happening, he quickly pulled her closer to him, as though he was trying to send me a definite message. My dad had a bag lunch and offered me half. I didn't bring any because I didn't think that I would be in the mood for anything, and I wasn't. I just wanted to be away from there as long a possible, so we drove around and my dad ate his sandwich under a tree in a churchyard.

Recess soon ended and we went back to our respective seclusion at the courthouse. I was not recalled to the stand. In the back hallway, Lana asked me if I still drank. I said, "A little." Jerry said, "Yea, right!" Because I was drunk all of the time, whenever I was around him in the past. I told them that I *had* to be drunk to do what I did to my friends.

Dinnertime arrived and the trial was still going on. The prosecution witnesses received complimentary pizza and sodas. The defense witnesses had dinner on their own. My dad went to Hardee's™ with my probation officer, Ms. Poe. When they returned we all had a few minutes to hang around on the courthouse lawn before court would reconvene. This turned out to be especially awkward for me because, even though there were "friends" of mine all around and some were standing very close to me, I felt that, emotionally, we were miles from each other. Once again, the reality of what I had done to them was overpowering me and now there was no one I could turn to.

Soon it was time for the closing arguments and, this time, everyone was allowed to be present on the courtroom. The defense's main point was the "fact" that I was not a credible witness because of my history of drug and alcohol abuse. What the prosecution failed to point out was that Jimmie and I had been fast friends ever since the seventh grade and that, whatever I might have done that was wrong, he was usually right there, doing it along with me. The prosecution's argument was that "You can't get a preacher to buy dope." As soon as the judge sent the jury out to deliberate, my dad and I left and went home. It seemed that the handwriting was on the wall.

Later that night, around ten, I was curious as to the actual outcome, so I called Barney. When he realized that it was *me* calling, his voice became very loud and he appeared agitated. He asked me why I had made him look stupid in court and given the defense such an opportunity to make him look like a liar. I told him that I didn't know what questions he would be asking and, anyway, he and the rest of them had always told me to tell the truth. This did not seem to appease him at all and he said that I should have told him (what my testimony would be) so that his testimony could have been consistent with mine. He never did tell me the verdict, but it was pretty apparent, Jimmie had been acquitted. Against my better judgement, I decided to call Annette to see if, privately, she would understand what I'd been going through all day. It was instantly apparent that Annette was not home alone, in fact her mother and boyfriend were both there and listening to her end of the conversation. In a stern voice, she told me that I should not have called and that there would be no point in calling her, ever again.

Now that it was finally over, I felt no relief at all. In fact, now I was really questioning the whole point behind my priorities for the past year or so. My whole being had been centered around my love for Annette and all my efforts had been in support of our relationship and now even that has been taken away.

Chapter Eighteen

Reckless Abandon

By all appearances, my life had finally returned to normal. I had been released from probation and had paid off all of my fines. I was working every day, often seven days a week. I had established credit by opening a checking account and had enough money to make a down payment on a nice little blue 1997 Miata convertible. Of course, I had to pay through the nose for insurance because of my DUI conviction, but that was a consequence of my recklessness.

Even though it appeared to everyone that I had finally adjusted to my circumstances and was well on my way to a brighter future, it soon became apparent, at least to me, that no matter what I did I still hadn't gotten over Annette. It gnawed at me day and night, no matter how hard I tried to accept it and forget. Finally, I came to realize that life was no longer worth living for me.

I reached a point where anything that would numb the pain that I was feeling, even for a little while, provided welcome relief, even much needed sleep. As they say, old habits are hard to break, and before I knew it, I was pissing away everything that I had worked so hard for during the last year. The only time that I felt that I was even halfway coping with life was when I was drunk or high. I would go for days without eating or sleeping. As time went on, it became obvious to my dad that I was backsliding. This only made matters worse for me because I really didn't want to disappoint him all over again, but I felt powerless.

One day I was off from work and that night I decided to visit the bar at the restaurant where I worked and just relax and hang out. Of course, I could only relax by drinking beer, so I got totally blitzed. At some point I became completely overwhelmed by memories of what my biological father and other relatives had told me, continuously, as a small child: "You're worthless; you'll never amount to anything; son of a bitch." Now I was even believing all of the trash that Annette's mother had said about me. Maybe that defense attorney was right after all when he was quoted in the newspaper saying that I was incompetent, a drug dealer and an addict.

Suddenly it all became very clear in my drunken mind, I left the restaurant and stopped at a store and stocked up on beer. I would need plenty of beer-induced courage to do what I had to do. I got back into the car and started drinking one beer right after another as I was driving down the highway. My plan was to get up as much speed as possible and to drive off an embankment so that, finally, I could be at peace. When I got to the desired spot and drove off, the car became airborne and glanced off of several utility poles. Sparks were flying everywhere. The car came to rest after it sheared off one of the poles five feet off the ground and then landed on its bottom in the ravine. I couldn't believe it, I had just survived another wreck, and this time I had actually tried to end my life. I couldn't even get *that* right! I was taken to a hospital where the doctor was astounded that I made it through this without any injuries whatsoever. The state trooper who also came to the hospital was astounded too, because my blood-alcohol level

155

was .45 and most people start to pass out around .2. They called my dad and he came and brought me home. Not a word was spoken during the thirty-minute ride.

Later that day, Annette had learned of my "accident" and called on the phone. Somehow, she had surmised that it was probably a suicide attempt and was calling to ask why and to let me know that, even though we're no longer together, no matter what, what we once shared will always be there, but cannot ever be again. But she did leave the door open for possible friendship in the distant future. Suddenly I felt somewhat reassured and comforted by her words. I no longer felt the desperation that had consumed me earlier and also realized the part that the alcohol had played in deepening my depression. Maybe now I can really have a new start and get it right.

Now, after sleeping on the situation, my dad gave me an ultimatum. He told me that, if I wanted to continue living with him, that I had to go to substance abuse treatment or else I would have to live somewhere else. We had a long discussion about my options and decided that I would contact a friend of ours who works at a restaurant in Florida and to see if he would help me to get on my feet there, after all, I really did know my way around a kitchen. We called and everything was set for me to go there right away.

I would have preferred to take a plane to Florida, but my finances could only afford a bus ticket and my dad was not interested in fronting me any more money. We parted when I boarded the southbound Greyhound in Williamsburg, VA at 7:30 PM.

The End

www.ingramcontent.com/pod-product-compliance
Lightning Source LLC
Chambersburg PA
CBHW020433290526
45785CB00002B/829